# NOSTALGIA NORTH AMERICANA

## ARTISTIC PUBLICITY OF THE EARLY AIRLINES

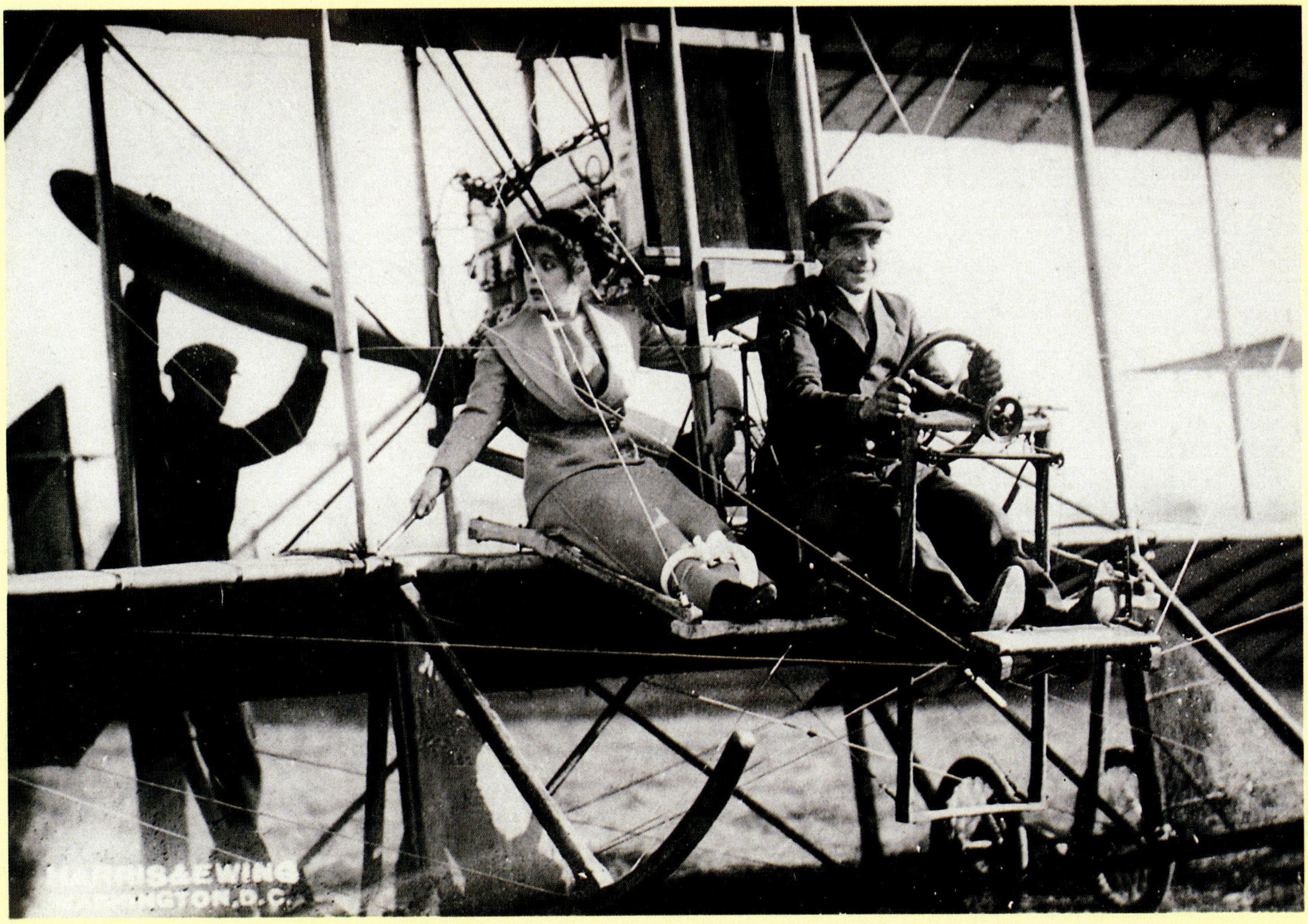


Alice Roosevelt, adventurous daughter of President Teddy Roosevelt, grasps the wires as Tony Jannus prepares to take off from College Park, MD, 1911, in a Benoist aircraft. Her feet are not tied to the plane – it is her skirt which is tied around her ankles so it will not blow up in her face.

---

Text and photography by W. Donald Thomas
Published in Dunedin, Florida, 1990
Printed in Singapore

## FOREWORD

By R.E.G. Davies

For the third time, I am privileged to be writing this foreword to a Don Thomas production, one in which he again shares with the reading public the joys of his collection of airline memorabilia.

These colorful reminders of a bygone aviation age are as much a part of its history as are the artifacts and aircraft housed in museums, or of the chronicle of progress as recorded by the airlines themselves. And these works of art, that characterized and embellished the early schedules, brochures, and publicity material of the pioneer companies, brilliantly supplement the more prosaic works of literature and the text books.

Like Don, I have long been a collector of timetables myself, for no other series of documents tells the story of airline progress more accurately, or in more detail. There were rare occasions when an inaugural flight did not go according to plan because of weather, the lack of aircraft, or a last-minute hitch in obtaining the blessing of the Civil Aviation Authority or a contract from the Postmaster General; but these were rare exceptions.

I would go further: in some cases — and there are several examples in this book — the schedules comprise the only documentary support for vignettes of airline history that were only briefly mentioned at the time in magazines or in the *Aircraft Year Books.* The timetables, therefore, are often the only primary source material now left to us.

These beautifully reproduced gems of the publicists' trade tell some of the history that the official printed accounts by lawyers and executives did not always reveal. The composition of the clientele of Colonial Air Transport, pictured on page 16, suggests that flying was an upper class mode of travel in the late 1920s, an aspect that is seldom mentioned in history books that too often content themselves with rather meaningless statistics and corporate details. The Ludington Line material from 1929 (pages 26-27) is a vivid reminder that the Eastern/Trump shuttle had a worthy predecessor back in the early days of air travel. The advice to the passengers in the Pennsylvania Airlines 1931 timetable (page 37) is hilarious, and the comment on the Maddux Air Lines exhibit (page 46) is an instructive social commentary.

Quite apart from these fascinating glimpses into the past, as seen through the eyes of the airline publicists, let us recognize also the historical value of the delightful pages portrayed in *Nostalgia Northamericana.* The 1920 Aero Limited (page 4) was among the world's very first airlines. Airlines such as Clifford Ball, Nevada Airlines (Roscoe Turner's "honeymoon special"), Maddux, T.A.T. (the other one), Wyoming Air Service, West Coast Air Transport, and a host of others: all these represent long-forgotten chapters in the glorious history of air transport in the United States.

Without these efforts, carried out with supreme confidence and a faith in the future, the industry would not be what it is today. To share Don Thomas's nostalgia is also to enjoy a flair for good old-fashioned showmanship that is perhaps lacking in the modern airline world of cash flow, code-sharing, and take-over bids.

---

Ron Davies is Curator of Air Transport at the National Air and Space Museum, Smithsonian Institution, Washington, D.C., and is acknowledged as a world authority on airline history. His books, *A History of the World's Airlines*, *Airlines of the United States Since 1914*, and *Airlines of Latin America since 1919*, are universally regarded as the "bibles" on the subject. One of his latest, *PAN AM: An Airline and its Aircraft*, is a complete illustrated history of Pan Am's aircraft and their usage. A companion volume on Lufthansa is now in print.

## INTRODUCTION

This is a companion volume to *NOSTALGIA PANAMERICANA.* However, instead of featuring flying boats, mainly Pan American Airways and its associates, as the first volume did, this book will depict some history of the other North American airlines, their predecessors, and their early landplanes.

Trunk airlines such as TWA, American and United have published hundreds of brochures and timetables, of which the early ones are already historic items and of great value to historians. The progress of these airlines, their mergers with smaller airlines to complete their route networks, their acquisitions of aircraft that could carry the mail faster, then carry more passengers, then ordering replacement aircraft with even more speed and more comfort – all these developments ended up in a race between trunk airlines to offer the best coast-to-coast service with faster, larger, and more comfortable aircraft.

These years of pioneering are reflected very well on the covers of the airline timetables and often on the baggage labels of the period. In the golden days of initial airline expansion, the 1920s and 30s, passengers did not often object to having a colorful sticker pasted on their baggage. Many of those who could afford the high cost of air travel were glad to show off their experience in that way, much like the travellers in ocean liners. The old baggage stickers that survived are now collectors items. So are the timetables. As a precaution against dispensing incorrect information, travel agencies routinely threw them out when later ones were received, and only the efforts of a few packrats have preserved these historical documents for posterity. The National Air and Space Museum of the Smithsonian Institution probably has the finest known collection of these timetables, which mirror the history of the airlines as do the labels.

The art work involved in the creation of these early brochures and timetables merits its reproduction in a book such as this. The author seldom had to refer to reference books; the information was right in the brochure. When needed, however, R.E.G. Davies' *"Airlines of the U.S. Since 1914"* was helpful.

All the early airlines of the United States could not be covered in 64 pages, and because of the cost of color separations and the desire for uniformity in both size and price in my series of books, I have had to pass up many items of fine material of interesting early airlines such as Embry-Riddle, National Airlines, Delta Air Service, General Airlines, Inland Airlines, Northwest Airways, Gilpin Airlines, Pickwick Airways, Rapid Air Transport, Mamer Air Transport, Varney Air Lines, Varney Speed Lines - there are dozens more. There are also the pioneer airlines of Canada and Mexico, all with interesting stories and colorful publicity.

I would like to share the beauty and fascination of this airline publicity with others who may appreciate the efforts of the early airlines to sell to the public the safety and convenience of air travel. I hope that this book gives the reader as much pleasure as it gave the author in putting it together. I have other books in mind.....

---

Unless otherwise indicated, all material is from the author's collection.

Collectors of airline memorabilia may be interested in joining the World Airline Historical Society, 3381 Apple Tree Lane, Erlanger, KY., 41018, or the Aeronautical & Air Label Collectors Club, AFA, Box 1239, Elgin, I11., 60121-1239. Each organization publishes a large quarterly magazine. The WAHS sponsors conventions and shows to buy, sell, and trade airline collector items; the AFA runs quarterly auctions of similar material.

Many thanks to Winston Williams for advice and assistance in photography and to Ron Davies for his considerable help in proof-reading and copy-editing the text. Back cover from Cheryl Ganz collection.

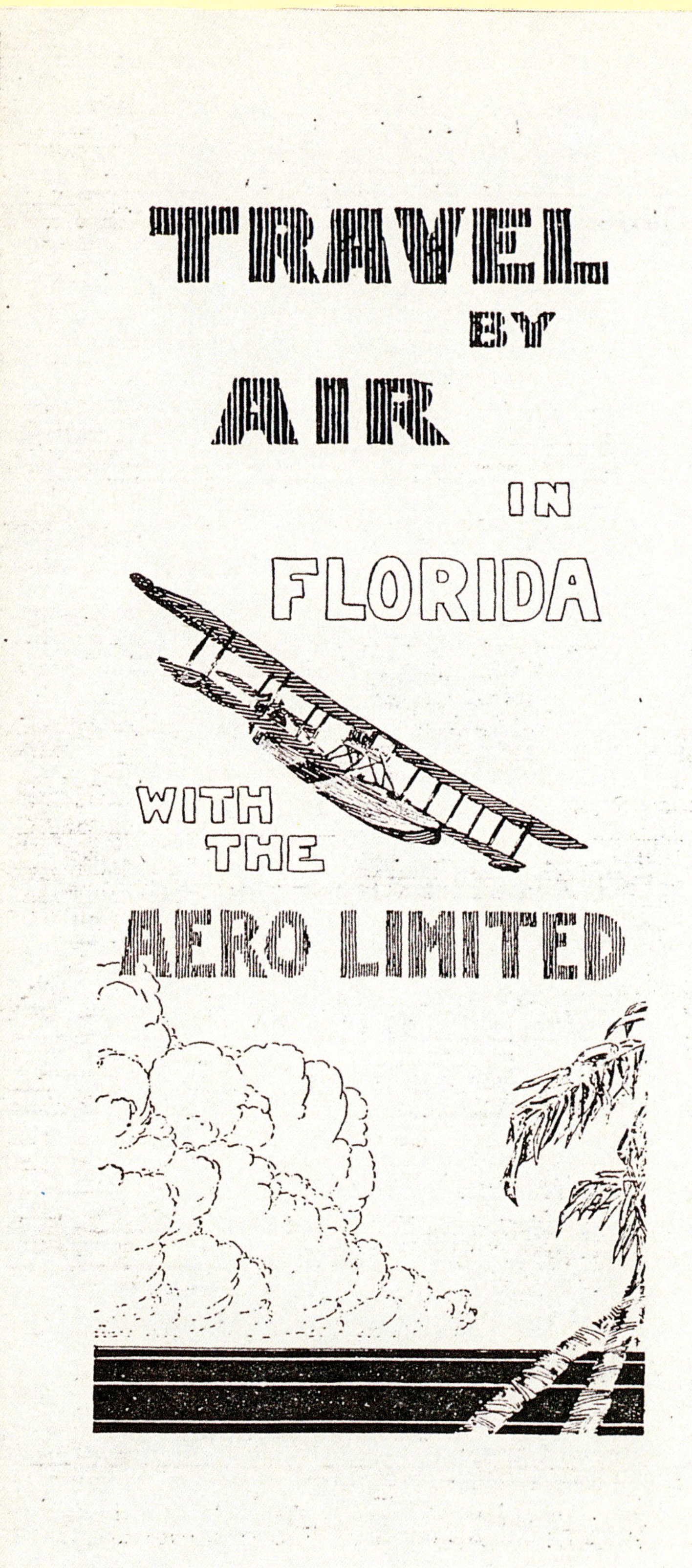


The latest in air travel – speed 70 miles per hour. $1.00 per mile was the cost for the three-hour trip from Miami to Nassau – about $360.00 for the round-trip flight. That was a lot of money in those days.

This 1920 brochure states that in July, 1919, the New York-Atlantic City air passenger service was inaugurated, followed by charter and sightseeing flights in the New York areas.

In November, 1919, two of the Aero Limited flying boats flew from New York to Miami, with eleven scheduled stops en route so that the two passengers, representing the Waterman Fountain Pen Company, could deliver fountainpens to their dealers. After this trip, all the other Aero Limited ships were flown to Miami and regular passenger trips were conducted from Miami to Palm Beach, Bimini, Nassau, and the Florida Keys. 40 round trips were made between Miami and Nassau.

The airline used three-place Aeromarine flying boats and the converted Navy HS-2L flying boats which carried four passengers plus crew.

Aero Limited was eventually taken over by Aeromarine Airways.

**Newspaper advertisement, 1920**

In 1920 another airline, Aeromarine West Indies Airways, was engaged in flying passengers to Nassau and Bimini from Miami, as well as flying to Havana from Key West. During this prohibition era many of the passengers were either indulging their thirst or engaged in liquor smuggling operations.

FLORIDA AIRWAYS was organized in 1926 by Eddie Rickenbacker and Reed Chambers, wartime aces of WW I. Four new Stout monoplanes with 400hp Liberty engines were the main part of the fleet. The 2-AT Stouts were named *Miss Tampa*, *Miss Miami*, *Miss Ft. Myers,* and *Miss St. Petersburg*. The line was awarded air mail contract CAM-10, and carried more mail than passengers. For nine months it operated from Atlanta to Miami, but in this era most people were still afraid to fly. When the airline folded Dec. 31, 1926, it had had no passenger fatalities, but was financially insolvent.

**The photo above was taken November 25, 1926, on arrival of the Florida Airways plane *Miss St. Petersburg* at the dedication of the new St. Petersburg Municipal Airport, Fuller Flying Field. The girls were "Miss Tampa of the Air", "Miss Daily News", and "Miss St. Petersburg of the Air". During the great Miami hurricane of 1926 Florida Airways airplanes carried urgent mail and passengers, and rushed in doctors, nurses, and medicines.**

2944

"GO BY AIR"

PHILADELPHIA

SESQUICENTENNIAL

P.R.T. AIR SERVICE

PRT

UNDER MITTEN MANAGEMENT

Operating Fokker 3-Engine Planes

WASHINGTON

The inaugural flight of the airline was on July16, 1926. Fare was $15., round-trip $25. A mail contract (CAM 13) was awarded for the route between the two cities.

In 1926, during Philadelphia's celebration of its 150th anniversary with the Sesquicentennial Exposition, a streetcar company, The Philadelphia Rapid Transit, started an air service. Two flights a day were scheduled between Philadelphia and Washington. Two Fokker F-VIIs were used for the $1^1/2$ hour trip.

FOKKER

BERTRANDIAS

PARKER

MUSICK

DeWALD

PRIESTER

**The men who ran the airline are shown above. Anthony H.G. Fokker, who had direct supervision over operations; Victor Bertrandias, former member of Rickenbacker's WW I squadron, who was operating manager; his assistant, Andre Priester, later to become famous as Pan American Airways' Chief Engineer; Ed Musick, who had flown with Aeromarine and was to become PAA's senior pilot; Lt. Parker, formerly with Byrd and Bennett on their polar flight; and Dewald, former U.S. airmail pilot.**

The airline was popular with passengers, in spite of the somewhat noisy aircraft, which lacked the sound-proofing of modern airliners.

In September a third Fokker was added to the fleet and a schedule to Norfolk, Virginia, was inaugurated. (CAM 15). The extra aircraft now allowed three round trips per day to be flown.

The brochure/timetable at left includes the Norfolk schedules and fares. Inside, the safety and comfort of the aircraft are described, with little reference to the pilots, except that they were all "carefully seasoned flyers". Speed of the planes was listed as 90 miles per hour.

The Fokkers had a capacity for eight passengers, plus pilot and "his assistant", according to the brochure. Apparently the word "co-pilot" had not yet come into general use.

The cabins were spacious and had picture windows and roomy upholstered chairs. Cabin space was more than we have on our modern airliners, which may be one reason why the airline did not make a profit.

When operations ceased at the end of November, 1926, a total of 3,695 passengers had been carried in $4^1/_2$ months of operation, without a single accident, confirming the airline's claim that flying was safe.

The PRT operation, almost forgotten today, proved to be a pattern for future air passenger operations.

Stout Air Services, using single-engine Ford-Stout all metal monoplanes, began flying mail contract C.A.M. 14 between Detroit and Grand Rapids in August, 1926, and had carried nearly 2000 passengers by July, 1927, according to this November 1, 1927 schedule of a later Stout Air Services company, the Detroit-Cleveland Air Line. After Stout abandoned the Grand Rapids route because of expiration of the mail contract, the Detroit-Cleveland Air Line was inaugurated, using four of the Ford-Stout monoplanes and two of the new Ford Tri-Motors. Twice daily flights were made. This line also proved operationally sound but financially unprofitable.

**Label of the Ford airline, which was used on Ford's Detroit-Chicago express service, which started in 1925. The label is dated 1931.**

Above timetable of April 1, 1928, is similar to the one which says "FLY to Detroit in 150 minutes", dated November 1, 1928.

Inside was the information "A roomy cabin, completely enclosed, in which you may ride in the same clothes you wear on the street".

These Ford Tri-Motors, although noisy, were roomy, and had, according to the brochure, "clear plate-glass windows which may be opened if you wish. Restful chairs from which you gaze at the wonderful scene below". Modern jets should have it so good. (National Air and Space Museum collection)

Colorful timetables, like this one of November 1, 1929, were issued every few months in 1929 and 1930 by Stout Air Lines, in colors like silver and blue, gold and green, gold and orange, or red and light green, like this one.

A plea inside to "Make the Trip by Plane" ends with "As you near the Airport of your destination and the plane glides the last few miles without power you say to yourself, "I have had a wonderful experience. This surely is the way to travel." Over 95,635 Stout Air Line passengers have felt just that way".

This colorful THOMPSON AERONAUTICAL CORP timetable/brochure of July 15, 1930, shows their Loening amphibian loading passengers. A similar timetable of the same date advertises "55 minutes to DETROIT by AIR". The brochure states "midway in your trip you salute a sister TAC plane on its way to the city you have just left." Fare between Detroit and Cleveland was $20.00 one way. Six planes daily were now used, compared with four planes advertised in their earlier June 19, 1929 timetable, which was illustrated in *NOSTALGIA PANAMERICANA*.
(National Air and Space Museum collection)

In 1931 BOSTON-MAINE AIRWAYS was formed, with equipment and management supplied by Pan American Airways, to operate north to Portland and Bangor in Maine. Pan American then took over the balance of the route to St. John and Halifax in Canada. Pan American's desire was to familiarize itself with the northeast region in preparation for its transatlantic flight plans. That agreement only lasted for a year, but in 1933 Boston-Maine Airways resumed operations in conjunction with Central Vermont Airways. It was supported by three regional railroads, and it contracted its operations to National Airways, under a similar arrangement to the one with Pan American.

Amelia Earhart was listed as Vice President until 1935, and by 1937 the National Airways association was deleted from the timetables.

The above August 11, 1933 timetable pictures one of Boston-Maine's Stinson tri-motors. Later in the year as an alliance was made with another airline, "Central Vermont" was added to the airline name on the timetables, of which more than two dozen were issued before the name of the airline was changed in 1940 to Northeast Airlines.

Their route to Montreal was operated with Lockheed Electras, the 10-A.

**Baggage label. When the airline name was changed to Northeast Airlines the same design was used, with only the change of name.**

TAT started mail and passenger service from Dallas in 1927. This was TEXAS AIR TRANSPORT, not the better-known Transcontinental Air Transport. For the mail runs Pitcairn Mailwings, as shown on above mail timetable, were used. Mail schedules as far as Minneapolis and New York were given, and a new air mail service to Mexico was advertised. Passenger services were operated by the TAT Flying Service division. TAT merged in 1929 with Gulf Air Lines to form Southern Air Transport (SAT), which became part of the Aviation Corporation (AVCO) in 1930.

This T.A.T. Flying Service brochure listed its passenger services from Fort Worth via Dallas to Houston; from Dallas via Fort Worth-San Antonio to Brownsville; and Dallas-Fort Worth-El Paso. Connections to several railroads and some early U.S. and Mexican airlines were listed for the various stops.

A timetable dated December 1, 1929, has an almost identical front cover, but the name is changed to S.A.T. Flying Service, Inc, Southern Air Transport, Divison of the Aviation Corporation.

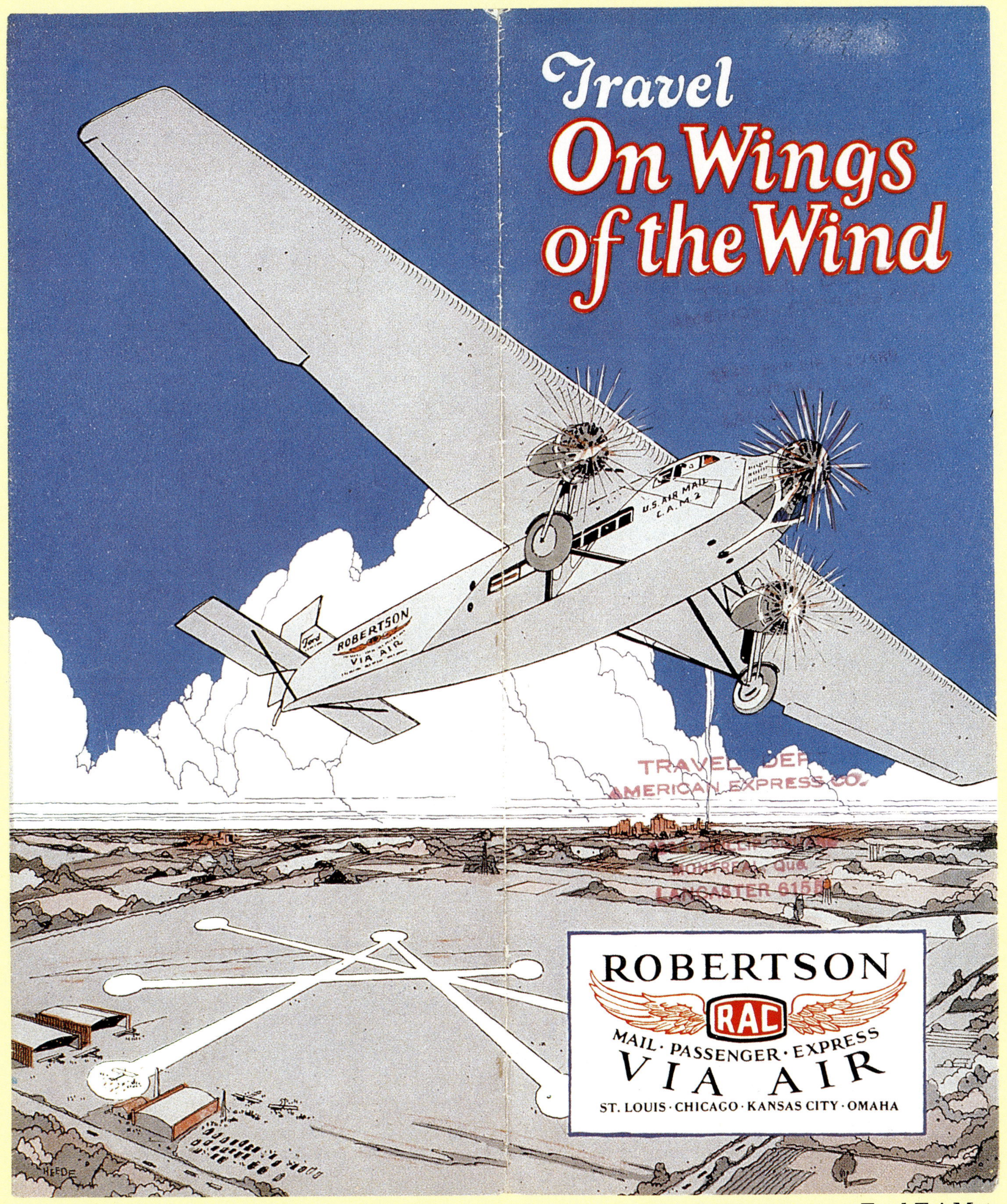


This rare 1928 brochure of Robertson Aircraft Corp. depicts one of their 12-passenger Ford Tri-Motors which maintained regular schedules between St. Louis and Chicago. This was the company for which Charles Lindbergh flew the mail in earlier days, although with smaller planes, and at night. The brochure declaims... "Come aloft, you earthbound mortals. For a few fleeting hours live the fairy tales of your youth. Sail the air in a brave, stout ship, with the clean wind blowing away your cares." For several pages it goes on and on, in similar phraseology. Universal Airlines took over RAC on December 31, 1928. In 1930 Robertson started another airline, "Robertson Air Lines", flying from St. Louis to Memphis and New Orleans, which eventually emerged with Wedell-Williams Air Lines.

COLONIAL AIR TRANSPORT started passenger service between Boston and New York in 1927, using Fokker Universals and Fokker Tri-Motors. Artist R.M. Goode pictures the prosperous-looking clientele which boarded these flights. Fare was $34.85 one way, a lot of money in the late 1920s. By 1930 the fare had dropped to $17.43, possibly because its passengers were not prosperous enough. Despite bad weather and lack of modern navigational aids, Colonial completed most flights, with no passenger fatalities, and, in the early days, sometimes with no passengers.

This beautiful 24-page limited first edition booklet was presented to passengers who travelled the skyway between New York and Boston. Very well illustrated, the cover shows one of the three Ford Tri-Motor planes which maintained the route in 1929. They were named *Nacomos, Nemissa,* and *Nonantum.*

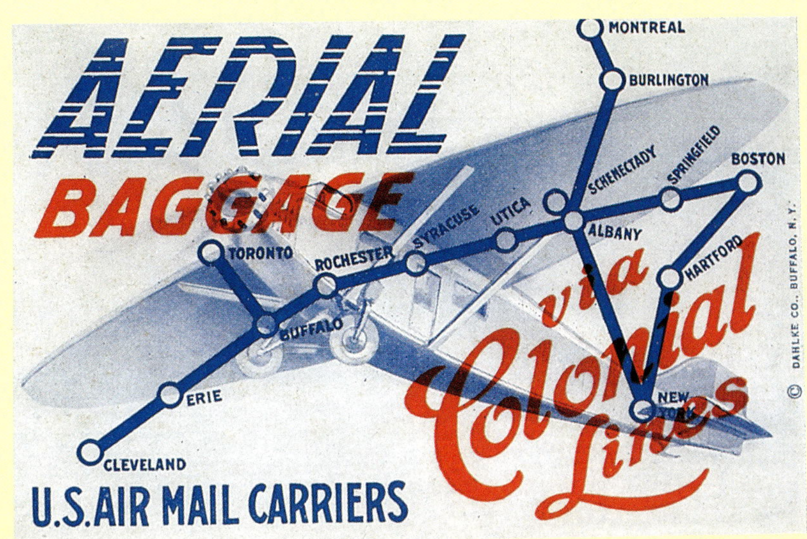


In 1930 Colonial Airways, consisting of Colonial Air Transport (CAM-1), Colonial Western Airways (CAM-20), and Canadian Colonial Airways (FAM-1), became a division of American Airways.

**On left, a rare early baggage label of Colonial.**

UNIVERSAL AIR LINES had absorbed Northern Air Lines, Robertson Air Lines, the old Continental Airlines, the original Braniff Airlines, and the old Central Airlines, with the idea of inaugurating the first rail-air-rail coast-to-coast service across the United States. This July 20, 1929, timetable lists all the divisions above and their schedules. The Aviation Corporation soon took over Universal Airlines and it became a division of American Airways, which was the operating company of the Aviation Corporation.

The brochure on the opposite page, describing "The New Era", says: "At the airport, Government-licensed planes, manned by Government-licensed pilots with thousands of hours of flying are waiting, the engines warmed up. Softly, swiftly you leave the ground. There is no sensation of speed – no feeling of height. Gradually your vision broadens. A panorama of scenic beauty spreads before you as you wing your way through the space. Fascinating bits of landscape slip swiftly by... Suddenly, the skyline of another large city attracts your eye. Before you realize it you find your plane rolling smoothly up the airport runway. A stroll, a delightful meal, and you're off again... Away with a smoothness only found in air travel. Up, up, up on wings of the wind. Exhilarating moments as you become inured to the feel of flight. You look down upon plodding mortals who travel with feet of clay. Sixteen or sixty, you thrill to your own participation in man's conquest of the air. All too soon comes the close of a perfect day."

Not like that now, is it?

The aircraft was a Fokker 10A

UNIVERSAL AIR LINES SYSTEM

"THE SKYWAYS—OUR HIGHWAYS" ©

Coast to Coast

by

AIR and RAIL

in

2 Business Days

UNIVERSAL AIR LINES
NEW YORK CENTRAL
SANTA FE

—1—

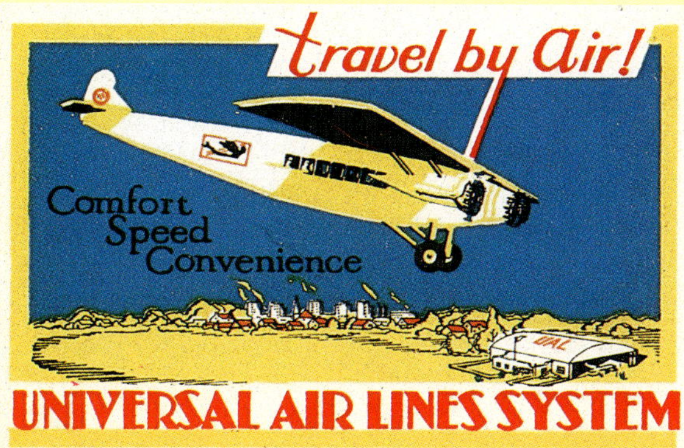


**Baggage label**

The timetable above schedules departure on New York Central RR on Sunday, arrival at Cleveland on Monday, transferring to Universal Air Express and arriving at Garden City, Kansas, in the evening, then transferring to the Atchison, Topeka and Santa Fe RR, finally arriving in Los Angeles Wednesday morning. Monday and Tuesday would be the "2 business days" required.

In 1934 American Airways became American Airlines, one of the four large trunk airline systems in the U.S. The others were United, TWA and Eastern.

A February 10, 1930 timetable of American Airways Universal Division schedules departure from New York on New York Central railroad trains to Cleveland, then by Universal Airlines to Tulsa, Oklahoma, then by Southern Air Transport to Dallas.

**AMERICAN AIRWAYS, Inc.**

**[Operating Company of The Aviation Corp.]**

**UNIVERSAL DIVISION**

**FARES and SCHEDULES**

*(Subject to Change Without Notice)*

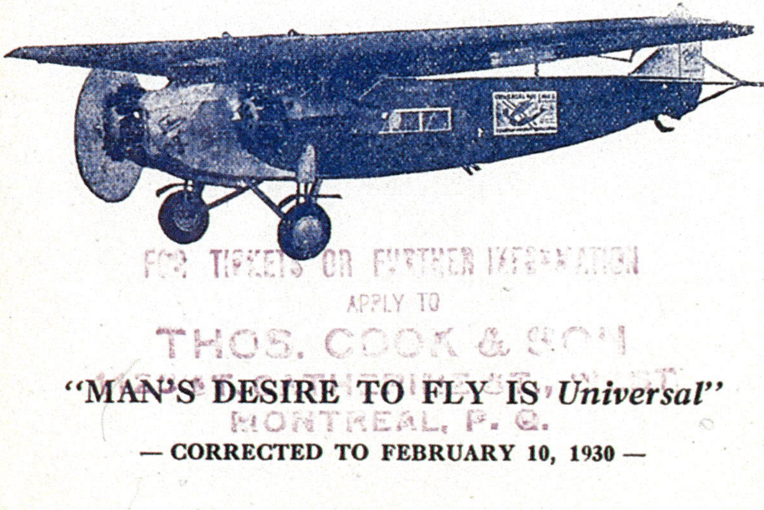


"MAN'S DESIRE TO FLY IS *Universal*"

— CORRECTED TO FEBRUARY 10, 1930 —

AMERICAN AIRWAYS, Inc., was formed in 1930, as the airline of the Aviation Corporation of America (AVCO). AVCO was a combination of Universal Aviation Corp. and Colonial Airways Corp. The latter had three Divisions, whereas Universal had combined Robertson Aviation, the old Braniff, the old Central, the old Continental, and Universal Airlines to form the Corporation.

AVCO later took in Southern Air Transport, Interstate, and Embry-Riddle, among other smaller airlines and companies.

**DAILY AIR SCHEDULE**

| | |
|---|---|
| AKRON | INDIANAPOLIS |
| ATLANTA | JACKSON |
| CHATTANOOGA | LITTLE ROCK |
| CHICAGO | LOUISVILLE |
| CINCINNATI | MEMPHIS |
| CLEVELAND | NASHVILLE |
| COLUMBUS | NEW ORLEANS |
| DALLAS | ST. LOUIS |
| DAYTON | SPRINGFIELD |
| FT. WORTH | TEXARKANA |

**AMERICAN AIRWAYS**

*Corrected to August 1, 1931*

*Standard Time*

This August 1, 1931, timetable with a Ford Tri-Motor on the cover, lists many cities, from Chicago to New Orleans and Atlanta, and to Dallas and Fort Worth, with daily flights. Direct connections by air are listed, to Los Angeles via American, and to other points by TWA, UAL, NWA; and by rail on several railroads.

The Universal Divison of American Airways is listed in this 1930 timetable as flying between Cleveland-Chicago-St. Louis-Tulsa, with connections to Kansas City-Tulsa-Oklahoma City-Fort Worth-Dallas via Southern Air Transport, and to New York and Boston via New York Central Railroad.

This beautiful 12-page brochure from the early 1930s was illustrated with many photographs of scenes along the routes, and pictures of the company's operations and aircraft. "For Swift Comfort – Go by Air" was the motto, and "Experience – Service – Vigilence" was headlined.

**Above, American Airways' first baggage label, now very rare, pictured an airway beacon. In 1923 the Post Office had installed beacons on many important airways, and by 1925 the lighted airway system was completed all the way to San Francisco, making night flying commonplace.**

**Most AA baggage labels feature the familiar AA eagle with outstretched wings, as below.**

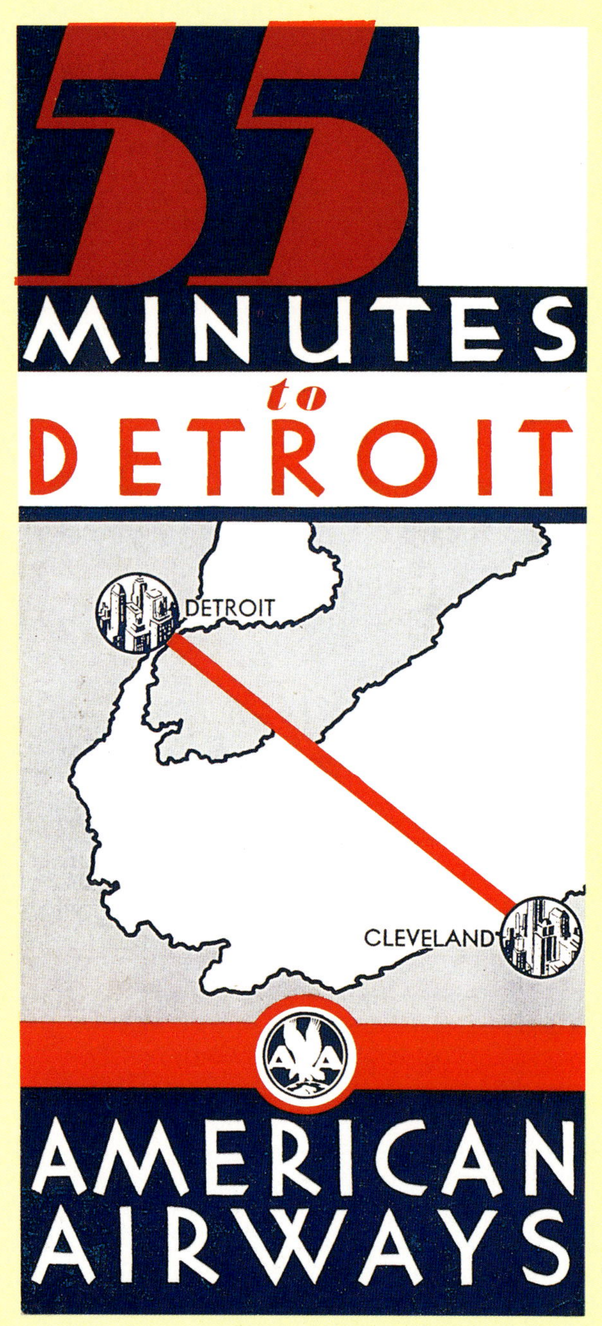


"55 minutes to Detroit ". This May 3, 1933 timetable listed a little-known overwater service of American Airways, using S-38 Sikorsky amphibians between Cleveland and Detroit across Lake Erie. Up to 1932 Transamerican Airlines had been advertising a similar flight of 55 minutes between Cleveland and Detroit, using Loening amphibians, so American Airways no doubt took over this amphibian route when Transamerican switched to landplanes on the run later in the year.

By June 1, 1935, Pennsylvania Airlines issued a special timetable covering this Cleveland-Detroit route, using 3-mile a minute Boeing 247s for a 45 or 50 minute service.

AMERICAN AIRWAYS CONNECTS 75 AMERICAN CITIES

**AMPHIBIAN SERVICE**

**CLEVELAND—DETROIT**

***DAILY EXCEPT SUNDAYS AND HOLIDAYS — All Times Shown Are STANDARD***

| READ DOWN | | | Starting May 3, 1933 | | | READ UP | | |
|---|---|---|---|---|---|---|---|---|
| 8:30 am | 11:30 am | 5:30 pm | Lv. | Cleveland | Ar. | 9:25 am | 1:55 pm | 6:25 pm |
| 9:25 am | 12:25 pm | 6:25 pm | Ar. | Detroit | Lv. | 8:30 am | 1:00 pm | 5:30 pm |

This direct, trans-lake route is in addition to the American Airways schedules between Cleveland and Detroit, via Toledo.

American Airways continued to absorb various smaller airlines, including Century Airlines, Century Pacific Airlines, Standard Airlines, Martz Airlines, Southwest Air Fast Express, and Transamerican Corp.

In 1934, after cancellation of the mail contracts and redistribution of airmail contracts which necessitated some revision of routes, the airline was reorganized and renamed AMERICAN AIRLINES, with no further connection to AVCO.

The Curtiss Condor, the first to offer sleeper service, was introduced on the transcontinental routes, as shown on the leaflet on left. In December, 1934, the DC-2 was added to the fleet.

In 1936 the DC-3 and the sleeper version, the DST, were put into service, and now American was able to increase profits because of the increase in passenger load with no increase in operating expense, compared to the Condors.

The small 1937 leaflet on right advertised these coast-to-coast sleeper planes. They were put onto nonstop service between New York and Chicago, and New York and Boston. 37 of these DC-3 types would soon be operating, according to the leaflet.

This 1936 brochure was a pitch to steamer passengers – air transport's advantages over rail or bus transport. 35 pounds of baggage was carried on the plane for free, and 100 pounds more by fast rail express.

In June, 1936, American Airlines introduced the DST. This brochure states "Only American provides the luxury of complete sleeper planes for transcontinental passengers". A year later TWA started sleeper plane service with the DSTs.

American Airlines operated a connecting flight to New York from Lakehurst, N.J., the U.S. terminal for the airship *Hindenburg*. Eighteen flights to North America were planned for the 1937 season. The airship carried 36 passengers.

The connecting DC-3 was waiting in the background, as depicted on this rare baggage tag, when the *Hindenburg* caught fire and was destroyed while landing at Lakehurst on the season's first flight. A similar oval gummed label was also available for the Zeppelin flights, but after the tragic accident in May 1937 supplies of labels and tags were destroyed.

**Note the flag above the cockpit on the DC-3. The flag was placed on A.A. DC-3s when parked. The co-pilot was supposed to see that it was removed before takeoff.**

The attractive leaflet on right shows German initiative in Transatlantic aviation even before the *Graf Zeppelin* and *Hindenburg*. The leaflet, dated April 10, 1934, gave ship-to-shore mail closing times for the summer season, and claimed successful operation of the catapult airmail system for the previous five years from the NDL express liners *Bremen* and *Europa*.

The NEW YORK–WASHINGTON AIR LINE, or WASHINGTON–NEW YORK AIRLINE, as is lettered on their Ryan monoplane, was the predecessor of The Ludington Lines. This rare 1929 undated timetable includes a map of the route, with 20 intermediate emergency landing fields. "The Safest Airway", it says. Four passengers were carried in these sister ships of Col. Lindbergh's *Spirit of St. Louis*.

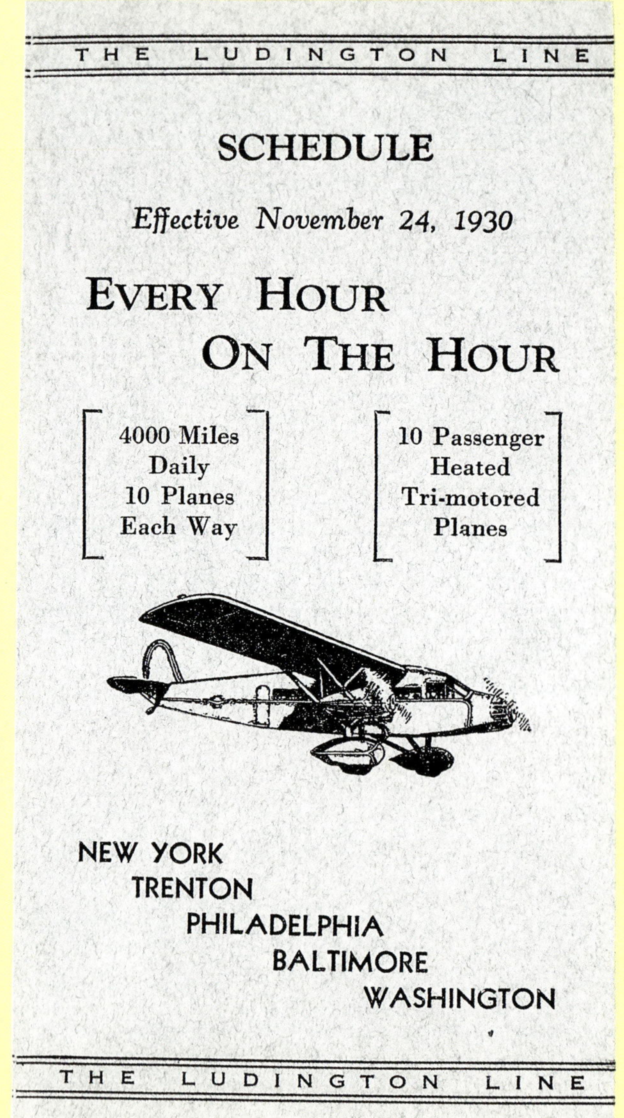


Above is an early timetable of The Ludington Line, which two months before had started a passenger service "Every hour on the hour" between New York (Newark) and Washington in daylight hours, 8AM to 5PM, with great success. At least 10 or 12 timetables and brochures were printed up to 1933, when a service to Nashville and Knoxville via Roanoke was inaugurated, under the name of Ludington Airlines of Virginia, Inc.

Although many thousands of passengers were carried with no problems, and a profit was made in the first year of operation, Ludington was unable to obtain a mail contract. In 1931 the government awarded the mail contract to Eastern Air Transport, which put the large 18-passenger Curtiss Condors in service on this most popular route.

In February, 1933, Eastern Air Transport bought the Ludington Line and integrated it into its own system.

This action, condoned and even encouraged by the Postmaster General, comprised part of the accumulation of evidence that led to the notorious Air Mail scandal of 1934.

**Ludington baggage label**

NEW YORK
WASHINGTON
ATLANTA
The AIR way

NEW YORK
WASHINGTON
ATLANTA
The AIR way

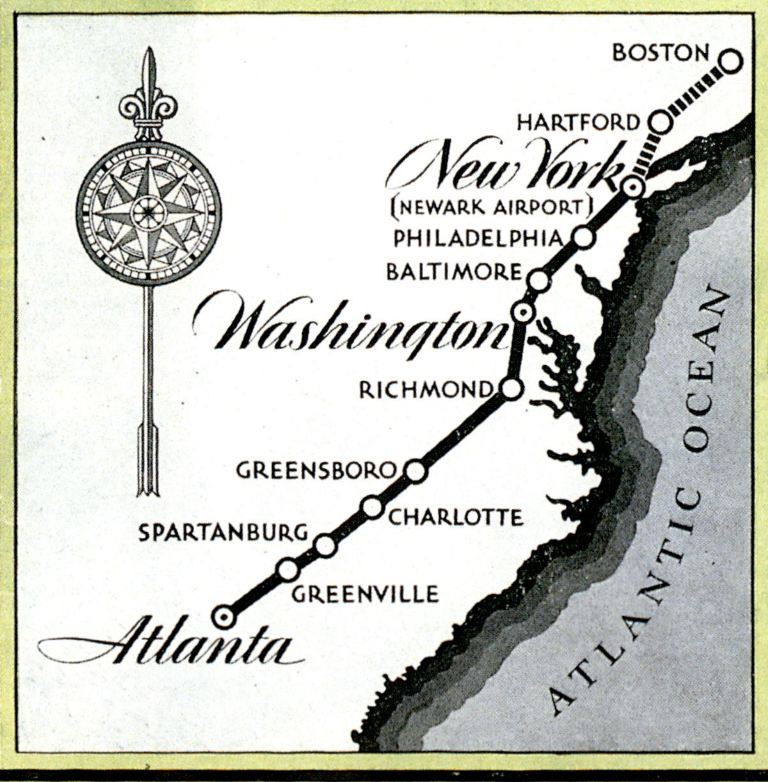

DAILY SERVICE
Stops at
PHILADELPHIA and BALTIMORE
Richmond—Greensboro—Charlotte—Spartanburg—Greenville

DAILY SERVICE
Stops at
PHILADELPHIA and BALTIMORE
Richmond—Greensboro—Charlotte—Spartanburg—Greenville

EASTERN AIR
TRANSPORT Inc.

EASTERN AIR
TRANSPORT Inc.

EASTERN AIR TRANSPORT was so named in January, 1930, after taking over from Pitcairn Aviation, which had been flying CAM-19 from New York to Atlanta via Washington and other points, and CAM-25 from Atlanta to Miami, in 1928. Eastern introduced Curtiss Condors on the New York to Washington Passenger route, and Curtiss Kingbirds on the route south of Washington to Atlanta.

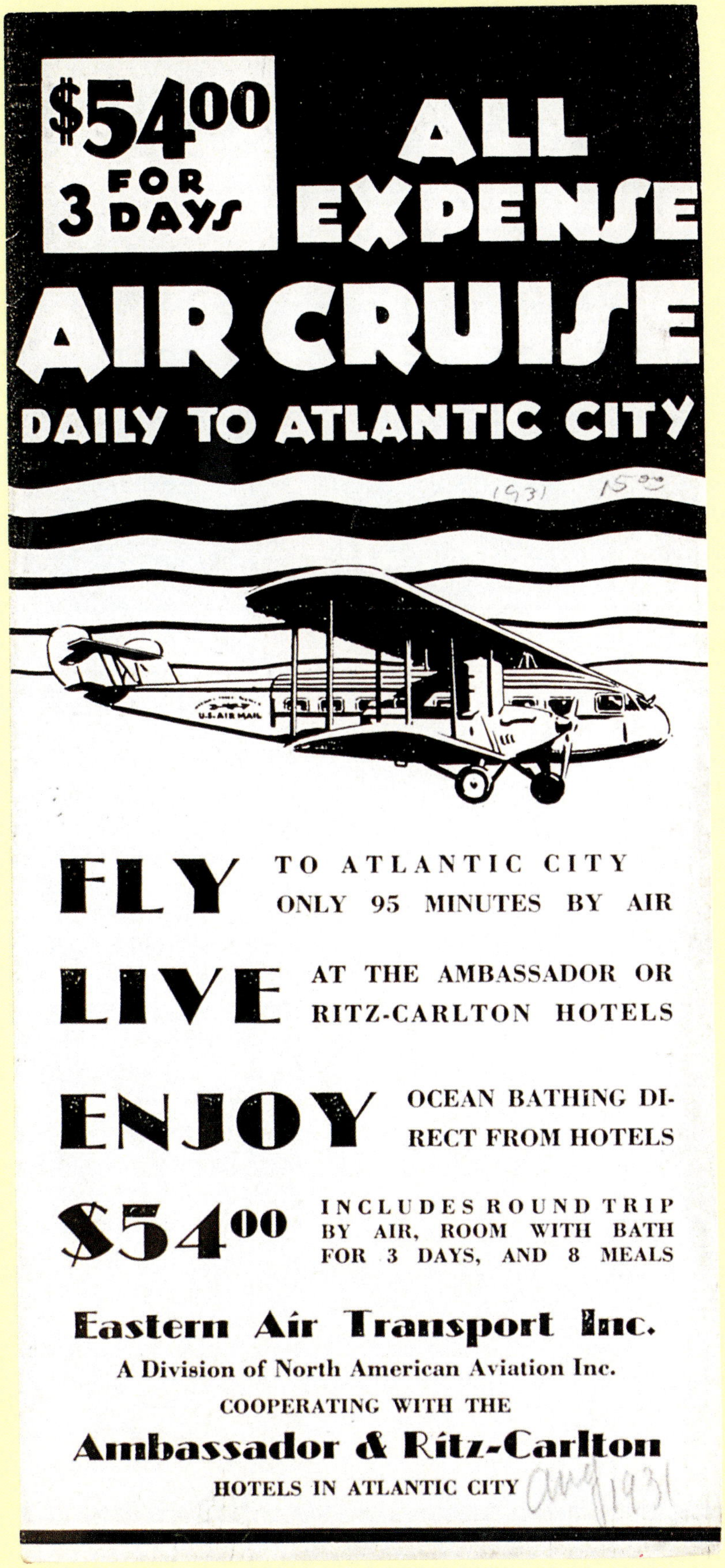
$54.00 FOR 3 DAYS
ALL EXPENSE
AIR CRUISE
DAILY TO ATLANTIC CITY
FLY
TO ATLANTIC CITY ONLY 95 MINUTES BY AIR
LIVE
AT THE AMBASSADOR OR RITZ-CARLTON HOTELS
ENJOY
OCEAN BATHING DIRECT FROM HOTELS
$54.00
INCLUDES ROUND TRIP BY AIR, ROOM WITH BATH FOR 3 DAYS, AND 8 MEALS
Eastern Air Transport Inc.
A Division of North American Aviation Inc.
COOPERATING WITH THE
Ambassador & Ritz-Carlton
HOTELS IN ATLANTIC CITY

This August, 1931 brochure shows promotion of the New York to Atlantic City flights, which were continued after the purchase of the old New York Airways from Pan American Airways the month before. The reference to North American Aviation Inc. betrays its affiliation to the General Motors empire.

Ludington Air Lines, in 1932, was the next purchase of Eastern, rapidly expanding its system.

NEW ORLEANS • BATON ROUGE
BEAUMONT • HOUSTON • SAN ANTONIO
Travel by Air
in comfort! save time!
WEDELL WILLIAMS
AIR LINES
NEW ORLEANS

Eastern Air Transport became Eastern Air Lines in 1934, to be eligible for mail contracts under the new Roosevelt administration.

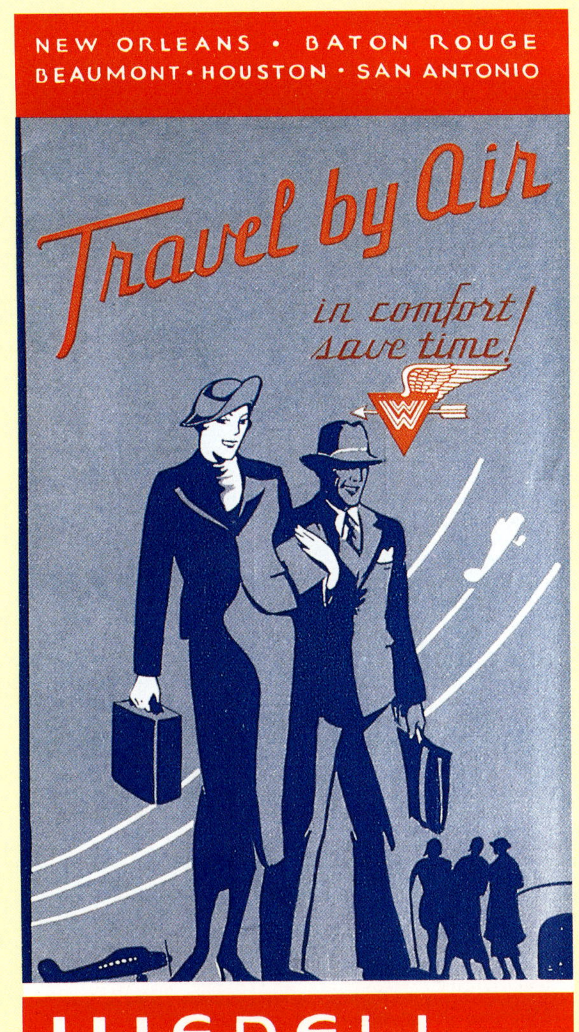

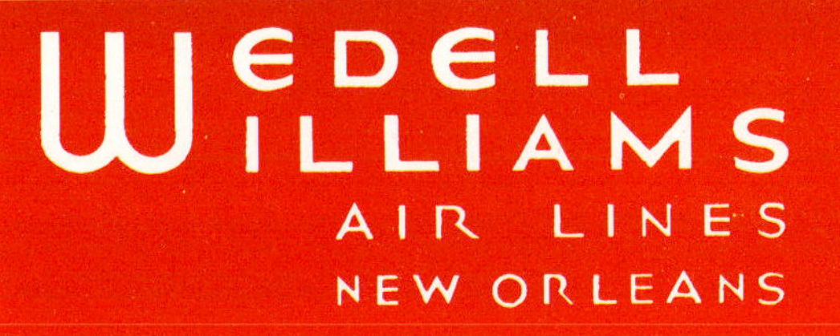

The purchase of Wedell-Williams Air Line of New Orleans in 1936 extended Eastern's routes to Beaumont and Houston in Texas.

Eastern Air Lines really took off with the advent of the DC-3. Although Eastern had been one of the first to order the DC-2, using 14 of them on the New York to Miami route, the DC-3 offered 21 seats instead of 14, thus increasing passenger loads and profit. Eastern had been using 8-seat Lockheed Electras before that. The May, 1936 timetable above pictures these "Giant Douglas Eastern Air Liners", and shows the DC-2 as well as the small propaganda labels used for the different flights. There were also labels for the New York Express and the Washington Express.

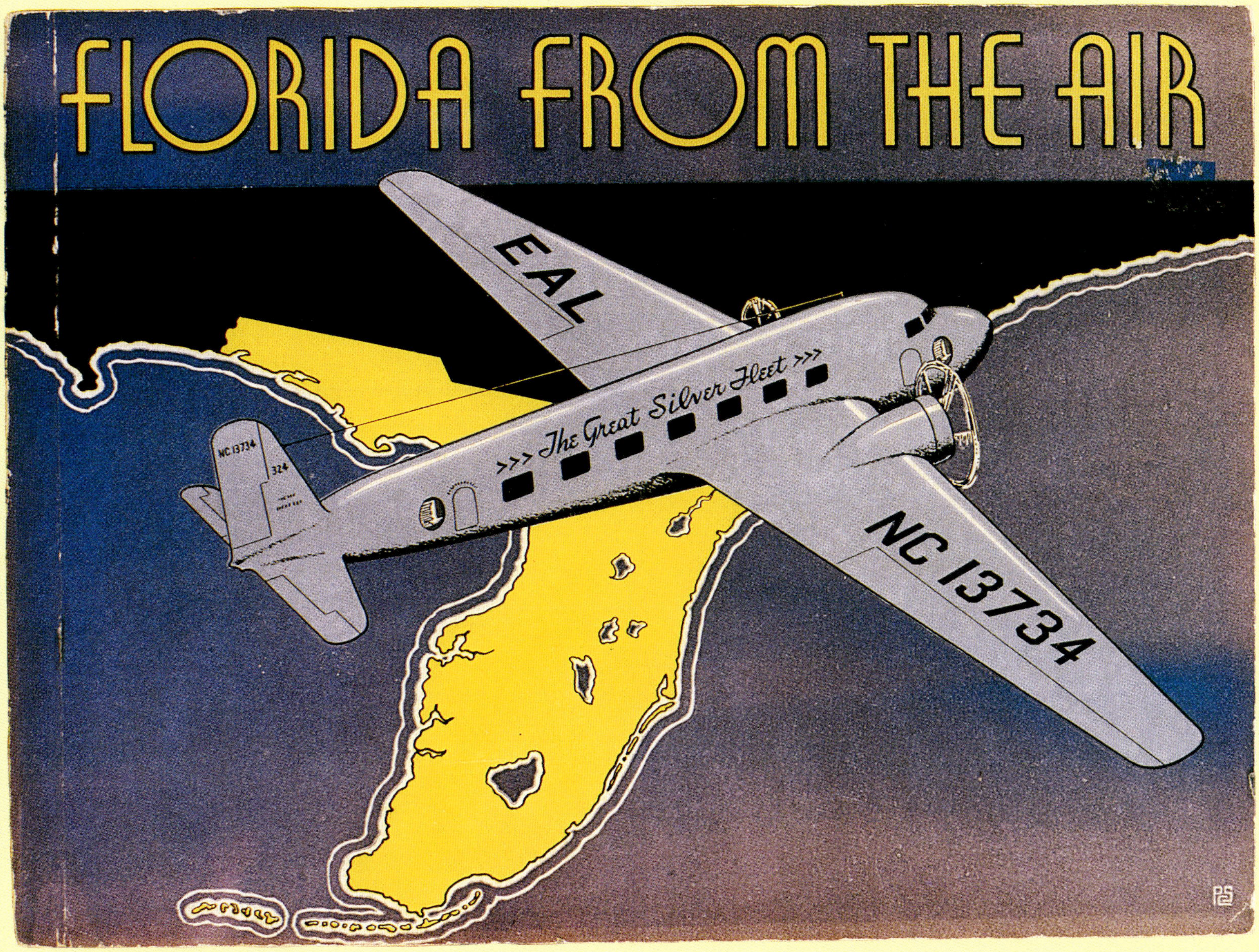

FLORIDA FROM THE AIR

EAL

The Great Silver Fleet

NC 13734

This was a book with 128 pages of aerial photographs of Florida cities, beaches, hotels, and other attractions of the Sunshine State. The price was 50 cents or $1., depending on the edition. It was sponsored in 1936 by various Florida Chambers of Commerce, the Aviation Division of the State Road Department, and Eastern Air Lines. Eastern was the largest employer of aviation personnel in the state.

**Stickers like this one advertised the fine fishing in Florida. Traffic was heavy. ▶**

**Soundproofing on the Douglas Airliners was appreciated by passengers who remembered the noisy Ford Tri-Motor and other early aircraft.**

BRANIFF AIRWAYS, Inc., was founded in 1930. It used 6-seat 150 mph Lockheed Vegas, as shown on this timetable of Oct. 1, 1932 and could bill itself as the "World's Fastest Airline." The main route was Chicago to Oklahoma City with connections to New York on United Air Lines and to Texas points via Bowen Air Lines and American Airways.

On the re-assignment of air mail contracts in 1934 Braniff received CAM-9 from Chicago to Dallas, a financial fillip to the airline. In 1935 Braniff inaugurated service southward as CAM-15 to Houston, Brownsville, and other Texas points, and put 10-passenger Lockheed Electras on the route. Bowen Air Lines of Fort Worth was later acquired, extending coverage to more of Texas.. Bowen also had routes to Chicago and St. Louis.

After WW II Braniff expanded rapidly, taking over Mid-Continent Airlines, operated a subsidiary in Mexico, Aerovias Braniff, and eventually acquired PANAGRA. It became Braniff International Airways in 1965.

**The Lockheed Electra 10-A was shown on this Braniff baggage label, which also came in a smaller size, as well as with the DC-2 instead of the Electra.**

Braniff Airways expanded through South America as far as Rio de Janeiro across the continent from Lima, and further south to Buenos Aires across the Andes from Santiago, Chile. In 1979 the Concorde was operated by Braniff under a special arrangement with British Airways from Dallas-Fort Worth to Washington, D.C., before the airline went into bankruptcy in the 1980s. Braniff has now reorganized and until 1990, flew a smaller scale operation before once again terminating service.

Bowen Air Lines
inc.
MILES AHEAD IN SPEED-COMFORT-SERVICE

DIRECT SERVICE
Dallas
Fort Worth
Houston
Austin
San Antonio
Oklahoma City
Tulsa
Kansas City
St. Louis
Chicago
Cleveland
Detroit
New York

Bowen
AIR LINES

Making a Neighborhood of the South

This March 1, 1933 timetable of BOWEN AIR LINES lists schedules from Dallas and Fort Worth to Oklahoma City and Tulsa. Despite the "Direct Service" list on front of the timetable, the service to all other cities was operated by either Braniff Airways, United Airlines, Transcontinental & Western Air, Trans-American, or by the M.K. & T. Railroad. The latter operated the segments to Houston, Austin and San Antonio.

Next year, however, according to 1934 timetables, Bowen Air Lines was flying all the way to Chicago via St. Louis.

**Bowen's Lockheed Vega is shown on the timetable and on this baggage label.**

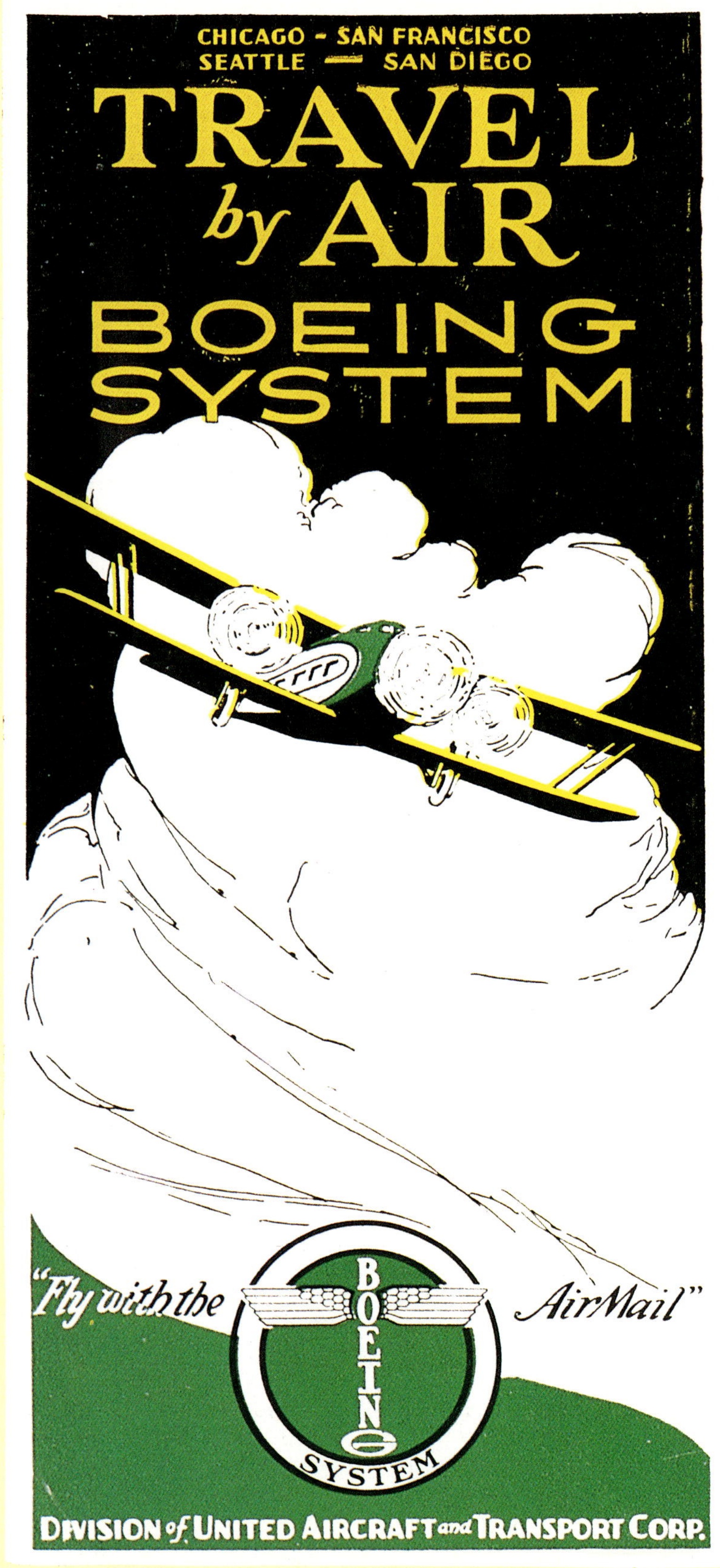


BOEING AIR TRANSPORT was formed by William E. Boeing and Edward Hubbard to fly CAM-18 from Chicago to San Francisco, over 1900 miles. Boeing 40-A biplanes were used, starting in 1927. The pilot sat in an open cockpit, which arrangement was widely accepted in those days as absolutely the only way to fly an airplane. The two passengers were protected from wind and rain but had limited visibility. They were supplied with blankets for cabin heat, and cotton for their ears (soundproofing).

In 1928 Boeing Air Transport became a division of United Aircraft & Transport Corp. This August 15, 1930, timetable/ brochure shows the model 80-A tri-motored Boeing aircraft which was being used by that time for passenger service.

**The Boeing 80 on an early baggage label, which lists the many important cities on the Boeing System, which included Pacific Air Transport and Varney Air Lines.**

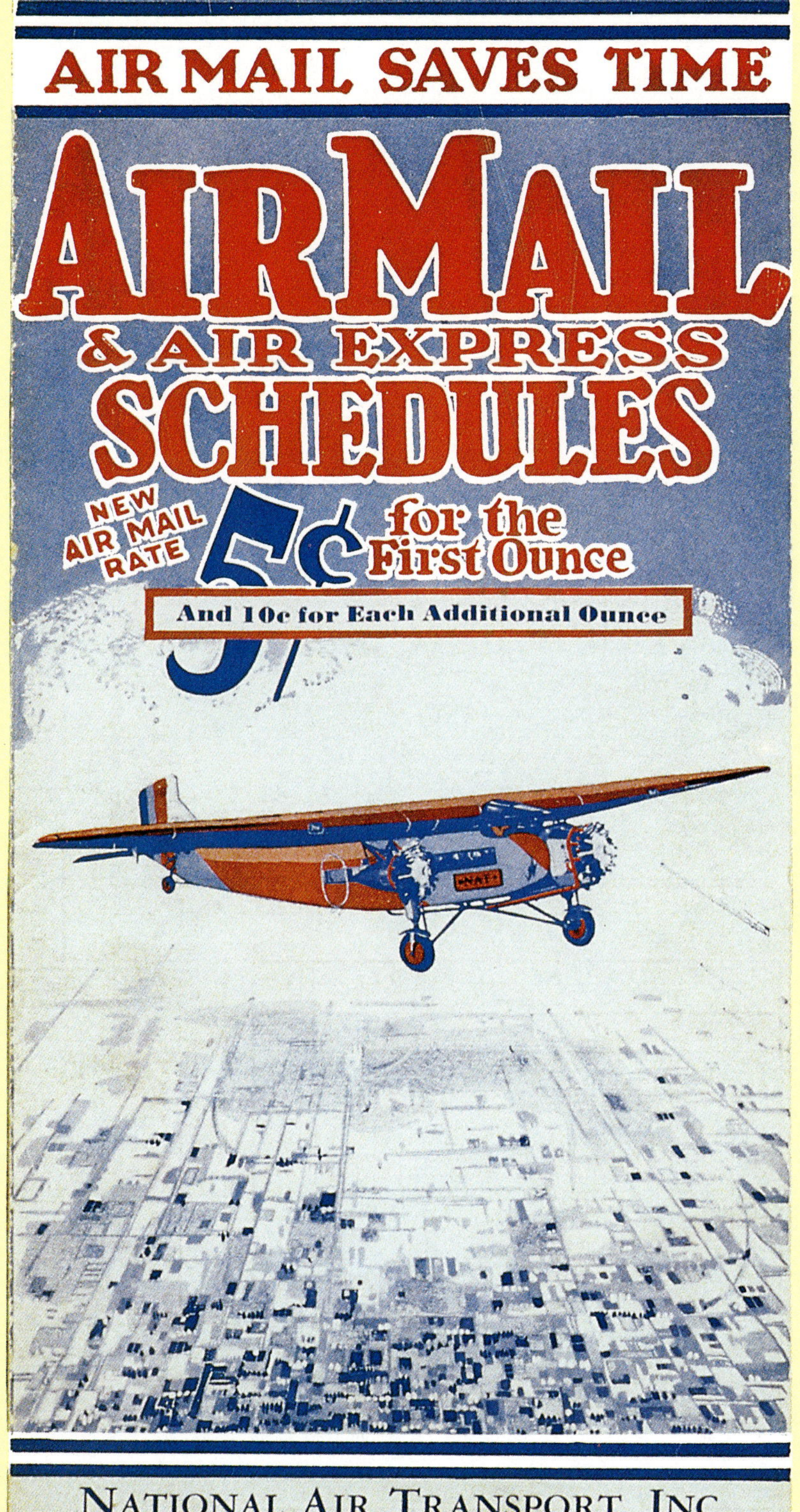


NATIONAL AIR TRANSPORT carried air mail and air express over the Chicago-Dallas route (CAM-3) since May, 1926, and between New York and Chicago (CAM-17) since September, 1927. These two lucrative mail routes made N.A.T. one of the more successful early airlines.

This May 1, 1929, airmail and air express timetable gives complete airmail schedules for all airlines in the U.S., with map of the routes. One of N.A.T.'s Ford Tri-Motors is shown on the timetable, although Douglas M-3s and Travelair monoplanes were mostly used for the early mail runs. Later, coast-to-coast passenger service was offered in conjunction with Boeing Air Transport, with interchange at Chicago.

In July, 1931, N.A.T. and Boeing Air Transport formally merged to become United Air Lines. Pacific Air Transport and Varney Air Lines had earlier been acquired by Boeing and were now Divisions of United Aircraft & Transport Corp.

**This beautiful baggage label is rare. It depicts one of N.A.T.'s Travel Air planes used on the early mail runs, with limited passenger service on the Chicago-New York section. "Limited" meant that only one passenger could be carried in addition to the mail and express, and he could be bumped in favor of mail.**

## On the Wings of the Wind

MODERN business and modern sport alike demand SPEED. To get from place to place in the minimum space of time has been the ambition of man since first transportation assumed any importance in his affairs. The airplane makes travel not only speedy but comfortable . . . No dust, no smoke, no cramped position or uncomfortable chairs . . . The thrill of hundred-mile-an-hour gait in perfect comfort, scenic possibilities never before equalled — and total time from Cleveland to Washington *Three Hours.*

CLIFFORD BALL *Inc.*

McKNIGHT, ROBINSON & CO. *Advertising*

BY THE PATH OF THE EAGLE

NC47412

CLEVELAND PITTSBURGH WASHINGTON

CLIFFORD BALL, INC., was based in Pittsburgh, and started flying mail in 1927. In 1928 a Ryan monoplane, similar to Charles Lindbergh's famous *Spirit of St. Louis,* was used for passenger service, and soon some Fairchilds were added, as shown on the May 15, 1930, timetable/brochure above.

In late 1930 Clifford Ball became Pennsylvania Airlines, which merged with Central Airlines in 1936 to become Pennsylvania Central Airlines (PCA). In 1948 the name Capital Airlines was adopted, and in 1961 it was absorbed by United Air Lines.

This undated timetable of 1931 was issued after the takeover by new owners of the Clifford Ball airline, and consequent change of name to Pennsylvania Airlines.

The inside of this timetable/brochure includes much advice on "If it is your first trip by air..." It states "For a moment you continue climbing gently in the direction of takeoff, and then the pilot turns the plane toward its destination."

"An airplane is handled in much the same fashion as a bicycle, so do not be concerned when, in turning, the airplane tips gently inwards, or "banks" as it is called, a normal maneuver, and, in fact, the only way to make a perfect turn. An airplane must be banked when making a turn in order to prevent skidding."

It then cautions the passenger – "Do not try to balance the plane by climbing up on the high side, but relax to the motion."

**Old baggage label of Pennsylvania Airlines**

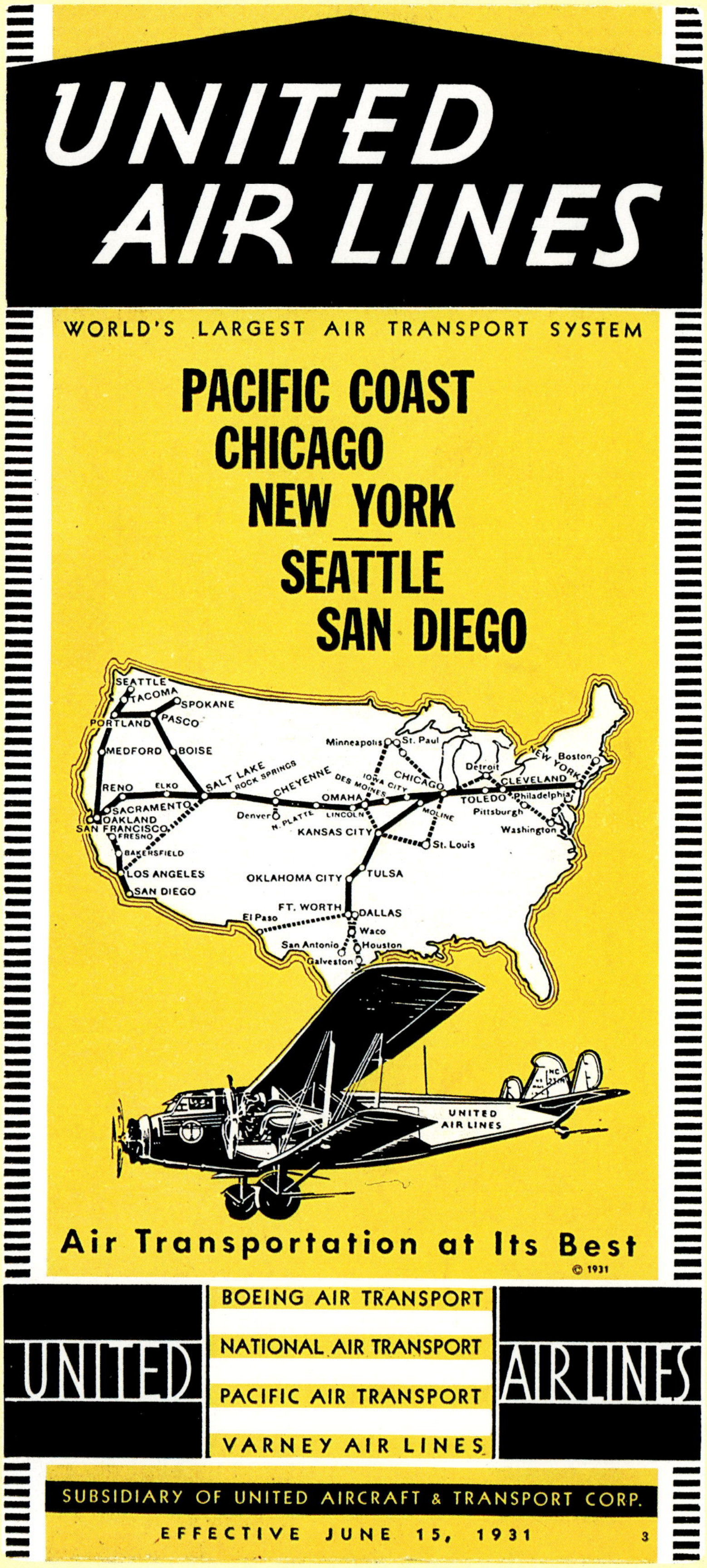

UNITED AIR LINES

WORLD'S LARGEST AIR TRANSPORT SYSTEM

PACIFIC COAST
CHICAGO
NEW YORK
SEATTLE
SAN DIEGO

Air Transportation at Its Best

© 1931

UNITED AIR LINES

BOEING AIR TRANSPORT
NATIONAL AIR TRANSPORT
PACIFIC AIR TRANSPORT
VARNEY AIR LINES

SUBSIDIARY OF UNITED AIRCRAFT & TRANSPORT CORP.

EFFECTIVE JUNE 15, 1931

UNITED AIR LINES, which in 1931 had brought together Boeing Air Transport, National Air Transport, Varney Air Lines, and Pacific Air Transport, featured "Air Transportation at its Best" in this June 15, 1931 timetable. The Tri-motored Boeing 80-A is shown on the cover. 46 cities in 20 states were now served by the airline.

The 80-A had 20 passenger seats. A photograph on the back page of a 1932 timetable captioned "Complimentary lunches aloft..." shows two passengers eating out of what looks like paper plates in their laps, with a stewardess in nurse's cap standing by with coffee mugs on a small tray. In 1930 United had introduced the world's first stewardess service on its 80-As.

The cross-country fare was $160.00, and this fastest coast-to-coast service took 27 hours.

**United's first baggage label**

UNITED AIR LINES

30 MILLION MILES FLYING EXPERIENCE

NEW YORK
CHICAGO
PACIFIC COAST
KANSAS CITY
DALLAS

UNITED AIR LINES

Air Transportation at Its Best

Copyright 1931, United Air Lines, Inc.

UNITED

BOEING AIR TRANSPORT
NATIONAL AIR TRANSPORT
PACIFIC AIR TRANSPORT
VARNEY AIR LINES

AIR LINES

SUBSIDIARY OF UNITED AIRCRAFT & TRANSPORT CORP.

EFFECTIVE JULY 15, 1931

1

**The July 15, 1931 timetable above claimed that United had a fleet of 120 airplanes. United used the slogan "The Main Line Airway."**

In addition to the Boeing 80-A aircraft, United had a fleet of Ford Tri-Motors, as shown on the timetable at left. United had acquired Stout Air Lines in June, 1929 and when it won control of National Air Transport in June, 1930, it used Stout's Ford Tri-Motors on the Chicago - New York route. The purchase of N.A.T. completed the transcontinental route from New York to San Francisco.

The 32-page booklet cover, above, reduced 50% in size, with the B-80 tri-motor on cover, was well illustrated, and gave the whole story of the United organization. United Air Lines consisted of Boeing Air Transport, National Air Transport, Pacific Air Transport, and Varney Air Lines. United itself was a subsidiary of United Aircraft and Transport Corp., which consisted also of the Pratt & Whitney Aircraft Co., the Boeing Aircraft Co., the Chance Vought Corp., the Stearman Aircraft Co., the Northrop Aircraft Corp., the Sikorsky Aircraft Corp., the Hamilton Standard Propeller Co., United Airports, the Boeing School of Aeronautics, and others.

Billed as "The First Modern Airliner", one of the 247Ds finished third in the famous England-Australia race in 1934. It represented the U.S., with pilots Col. Roscoe Turner and Clyde Pangborn. That plane was later donated to the Smithsonian Institution, and hangs in the Hall of Air Transport at the National Air and Space Museum.

In early 1933 United Air Lines introduced the new Boeing 247, an all-metal "three mile a minute" twin engined monoplane which carried 10 passengers, plus cargo and mail.

According to this July 1, 1933 timetable, 50 stewardesses were employed on United planes. A photograph on the back page shows a stewardess, now in the cloche hat fashionable at the time, serving a passenger with a tray of food to be held on his lap.

The main spar, which crossed the passenger at about knee height, is not mentioned.

**One of the new airplanes, 60 of which United said were eventually delivered to them, was shown at the World's Fair at Chicago in 1933. In 1934 this little folder was re-issued, in orange instead of green.**

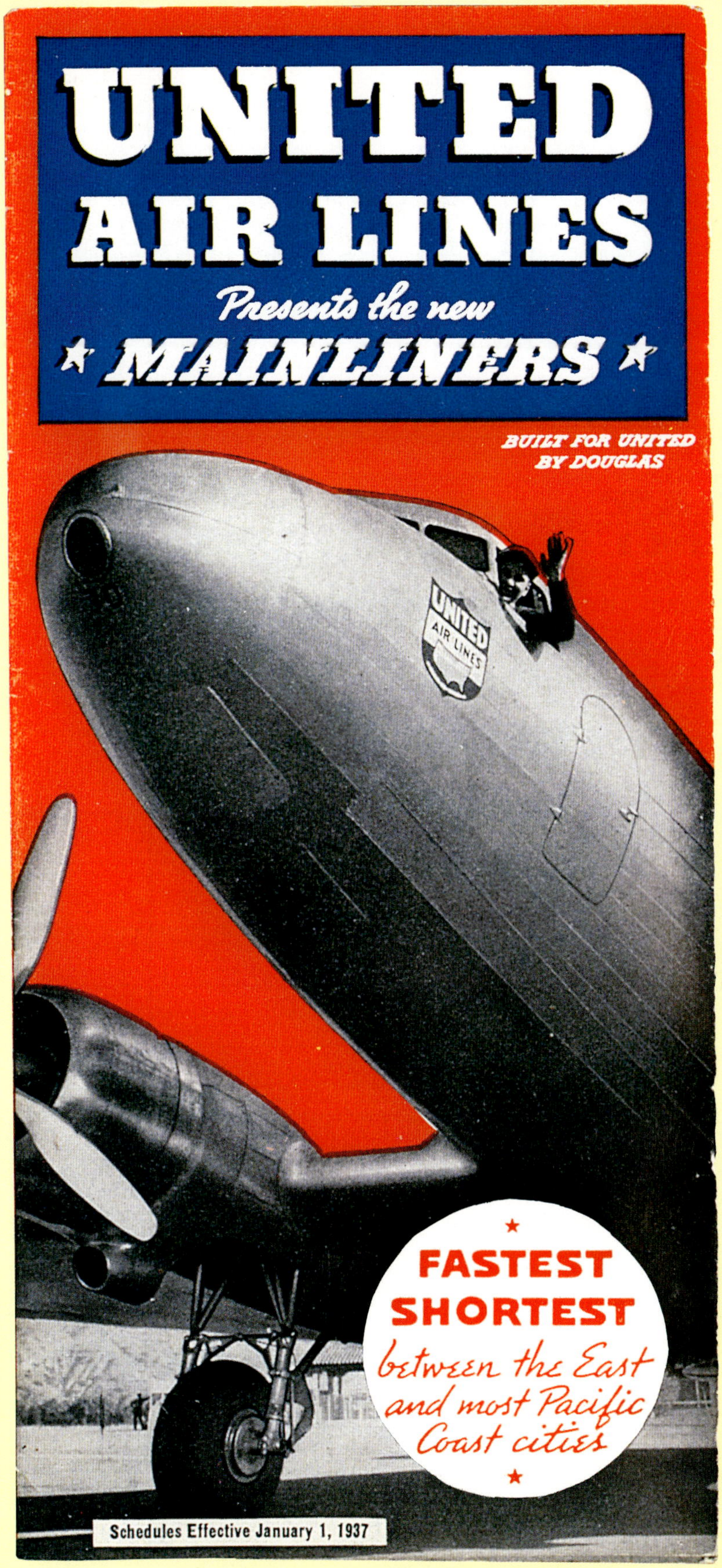
UNITED
AIR LINES
Presents the new
MAINLINERS
BUILT FOR UNITED
BY DOUGLAS
FASTEST
SHORTEST
between the East
and most Pacific
Coast cities
Schedules Effective January 1, 1937

The United timetable of January 1, 1937, which presented the new "Mainliners". These were DC-3s and DSTs in coast-to-coast services. Overnight sleeper flights followed by mid-summer. TWA and American Airlines were already using the DSTs for similar service, and had forced United to supersede its Boeing 247s.

Hot meals served aloft by stewardesses added to the luxury of flying United.

In 1937 United led the world in passenger miles flown, according to this timetable.

UNITED
AIR LINES
MAINLINERS

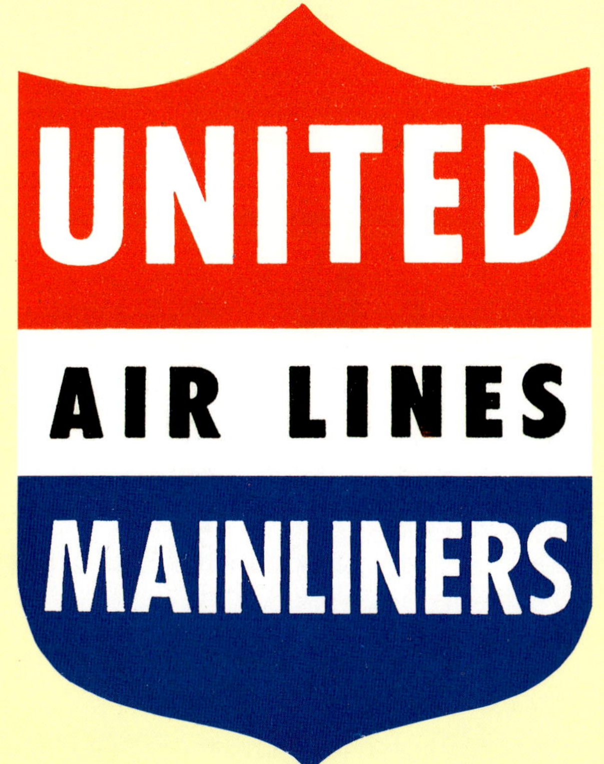

**The standard baggage label of United, which came in many variations and sizes. Similar labels were used by LAMSA, a United Airlines affiliate in Mexico, in 1943.**

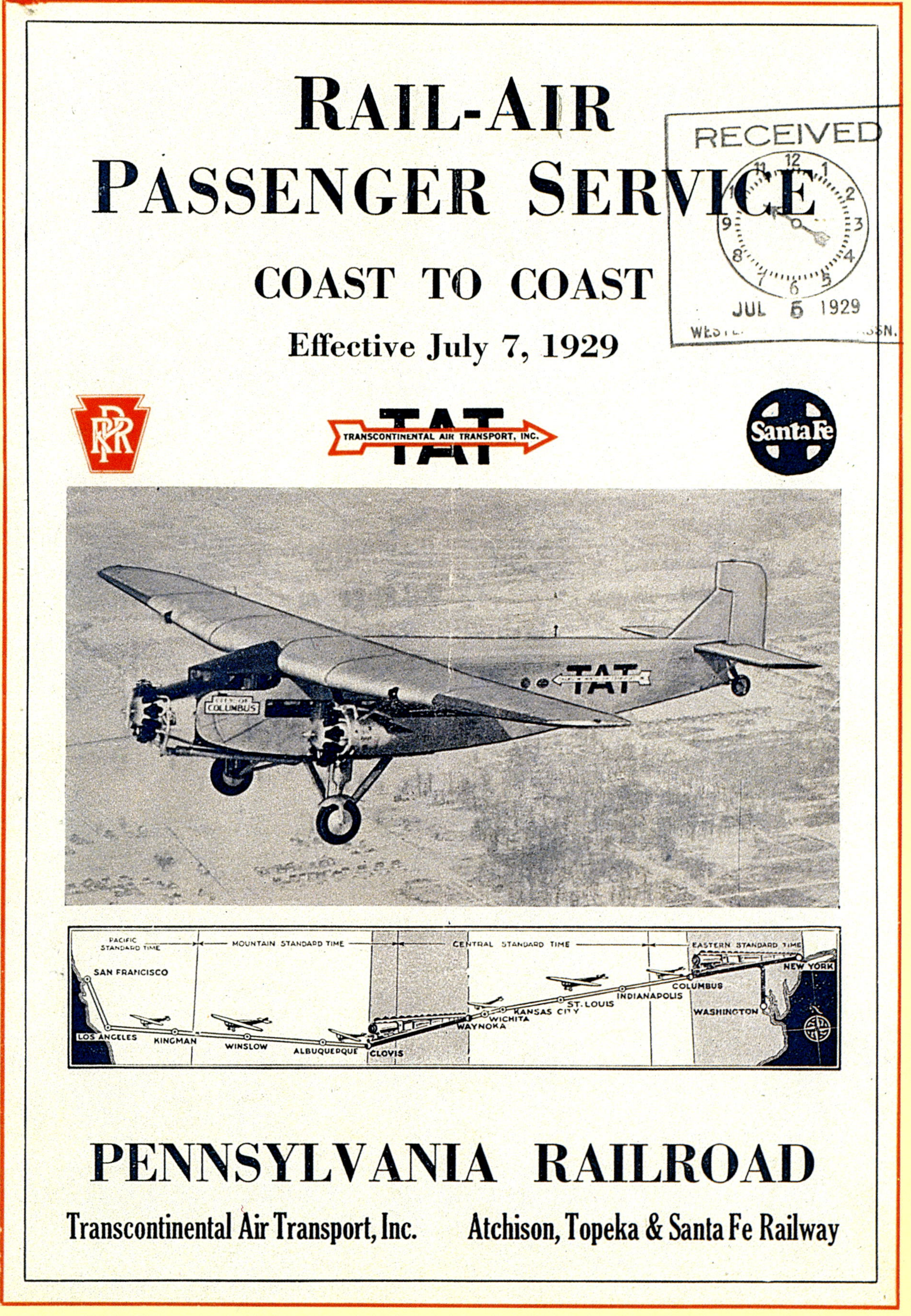


TRANSCONTINENTAL AIR TRANSPORT in July, 1929, offered transcontinental rail-air passenger service. The Ford Tri-Motor airplane, which could carry 10 to 16 passengers in reasonable comfort, with three engines offering an unprecedented margin of safety, was a boon in forming the new airline. Pennsylvania Railroad trains left New York at night, stopping at Philadelphia, Baltimore and Washington. At Columbus, Ohio, passengers boarded the aircraft for a day flight to Waynoka, Oklahoma. That night the A.T. & S.F. train took them to Clovis, New Mexico, where they boarded another Ford bound for Los Angeles Grand Central Air Terminal.

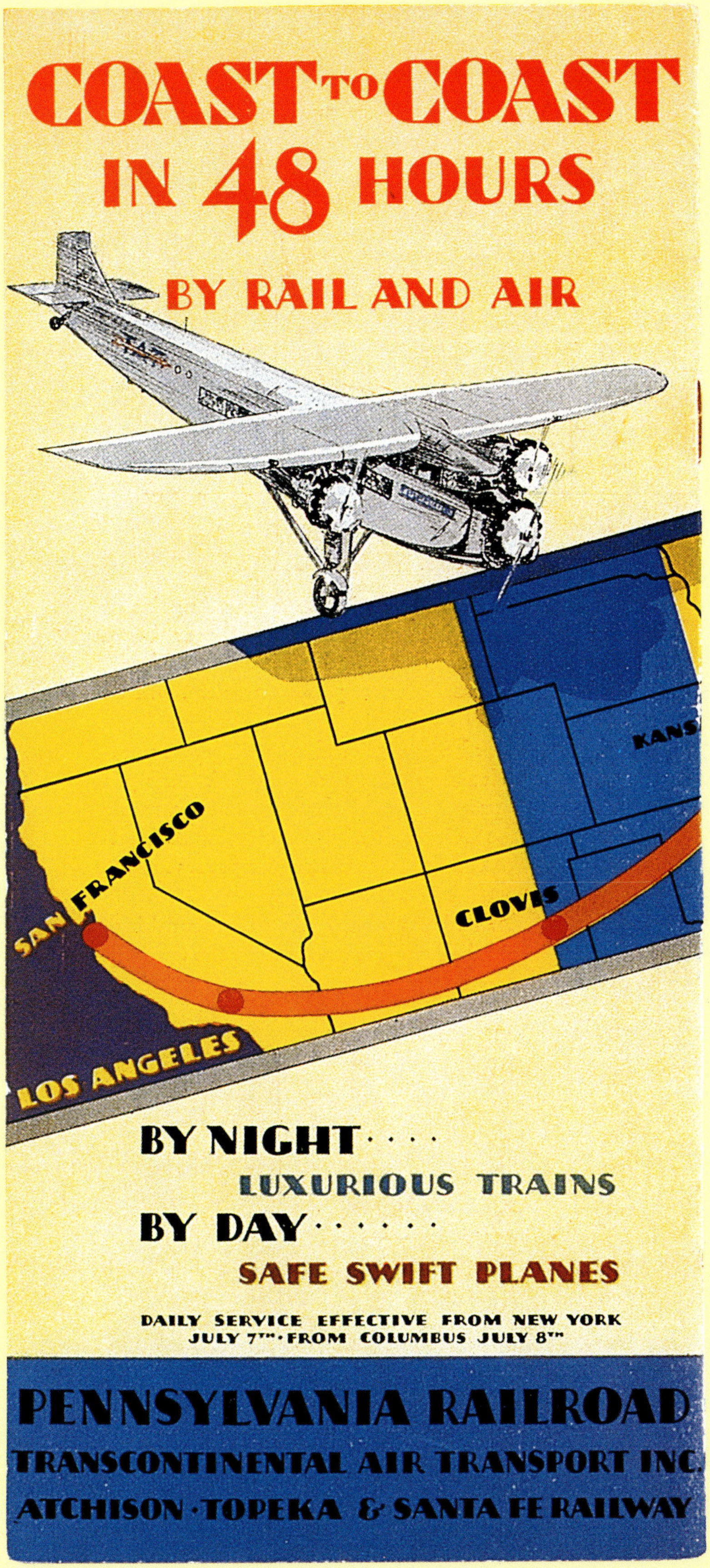
COAST TO COAST
IN 48 HOURS
BY RAIL AND AIR
SAN FRANCISCO
CLOVIS
KANS
LOS ANGELES
BY NIGHT....
LUXURIOUS TRAINS
BY DAY......
SAFE SWIFT PLANES
DAILY SERVICE EFFECTIVE FROM NEW YORK
JULY 7TH · FROM COLUMBUS JULY 8TH
PENNSYLVANIA RAILROAD
TRANSCONTINENTAL AIR TRANSPORT INC.
ATCHISON · TOPEKA & SANTA FE RAILWAY

At left, a TAT brochure of 1929. Large posters with this design were distributed to ticket agencies across the country. Inside, the brochure urged "from Columbus, soar like the eagle". 10 comfortable seats were waiting on the airplane.

Cost of the trip from New York to Los Angeles or San Francisco was $338.10, which included lower berths on the trains and transport by rail or air from L.A. to San Francisco. This fare would be equivalent to $4000.00 in today's purchasing values, and business was not as brisk as the publicity suggested. Indeed, the fares were sharply reduced in an effort to fill empty seats.

TAT
TRANSCONTINENTAL AIR TRANSPORT, INC.
COAST TO COAST BY TRAIN AND PLANE

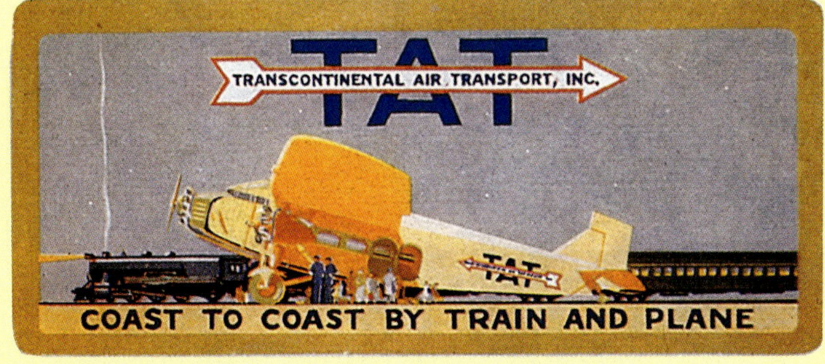

**Above, a rare baggage label of TAT, reduced in size by 30%.**

This beautiful brochure of TAT and Norfolk & Western Railway deserves a page to itself. The Santa Fe RR logo is also depicted. The train trips were usually at night, thru the dangerous mountain areas, and then the airplanes took over for a daylight flight. This brochure from the Smithsonian's National Air and Space Museum collection.

TAT
TRANSCONTINENTAL AIR TRANSPORT, INC.
MADDUX
AIR·LINES

Coast to Coast
by
PLANE
AND
TRAIN

MADDUX AIR LINES was a fast-growing airline flying between Los Angeles, San Diego, and San Francisco. It operated the largest fleet of Ford Tri-Motors then flying. Maddux was bought out by TAT in November, 1929, and the combined airlines then became TAT-Maddux Air Lines.

Despite its large investment and attractive terminal buildings, passenger traffic dwindled and TAT-Maddux started losing money. With the urging of the Postmaster-General, who was not in favor of competing transcontinental carriers each receiving mail pay, a merger of Western Air Express's Los Angeles-Kansas City division and TAT-Maddux transpired, in what became known as the Shotgun Marriage. A new company was formed, Transcontinental & Western Air, Inc. T. & W.A., which was later called TWA, terminated the air-rail service in October, 1930, with the first all-air coast-to-coast flight. One of the Ford Tri-Motors was used, with an overnight stop at Kansas City.

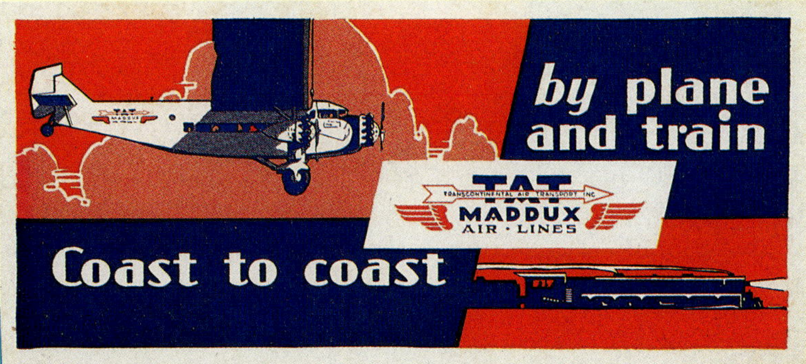


**Scarce baggage label of the TAT-Maddux Air Lines**

MADDUX AIR LINES, formed in mid-1927, operated for two years before being bought by TAT, successful operator of the air-rail route across the U.S.

This old timetable/brochure of August 1, 1928, lists the Los Angeles-San Diego and Los Angeles-San Francisco schedules.

Ford Tri-Motors were used. Maddux eventually became the largest user of the Fords in the U.S., with 13 of them. This brochure advertises "spacious accommodations for ten", and illustrates a passenger cabin with all women passengers. In those days it was apparently assumed that women were less eager to fly than men, as it notes "the number of women air travelers is increasing rapidly."

**Above, one of the two known varieties of Maddux Air Lines baggage labels. The other is in the San Diego Aerospace Museum.**

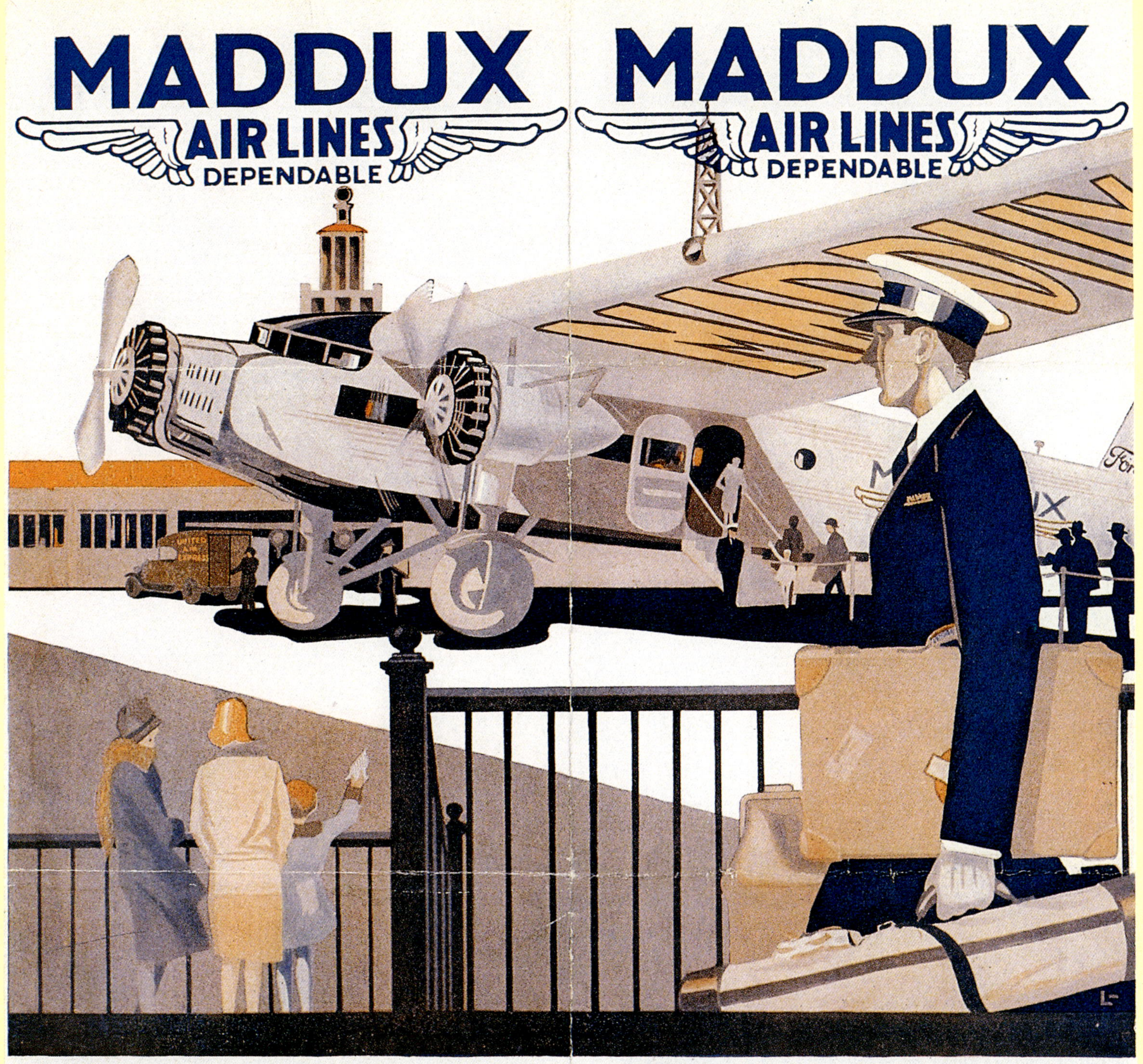


This 1929 brochure includes a map showing an extended route as far as Phoenix, Arizona. As in many early airline brochures, flowery language is used to allay any fears the passenger may have. This one, describing the end of a trip, says "... the airliner is making port. Your voyage is closing altogether too soon. Time does fly! Earthly contact is made ... no jostling ... no uneasiness." etc

In November, 1929, a major event took place -- the merger of Maddux with the giant Transcontinental Air Transport (TAT), to become TAT-MADDUX Air Lines.

In the early 1930s, when TWA inaugurated coast-to-coast all-air service, the Greyhound Bus Lines decided to get in on the action by issuing a joint brochure offering bus service from any of the points at which TWA stopped on its cross-country route. A 36-hour coast-to-coast schedule, with overnight at Kansas City, was listed, plus other schedules -- NY-Chicago, NY-Pittsburgh, and S.F.-L.A., all by TWA's Tri-Motor Fords.

TRANSCONTINENTAL & Western Air in November, 1932, introduced a new through service from New York to Los Angeles.

Leaving New York at 8.10AM EST, the plane arrived at Los Angeles at 9.53PM PST, a considerable saving of time over a 36-hour schedule still flown by TWA, but with an overnight stop at Kansas City.

**Old TWA baggage label**

The reliable Ford Tri-Motor was still being used on the faster trans-continental schedules. Note that Charles Lindbergh, who was the technical consultant to TWA, and who had planned the original transcontinental route for them, allowed his name to be used for promotional purposes.

With great fanfare, TWA had introduced the "Douglas Luxury Skyliners", specifically the DC-2, in 1934. This 12-page fully illustrated 1935 brochure lists and illustrates all the advantages – full headroom, soundproofed cabin, complete streamlining, retractable wheels, and many other features of the new aircraft. Its advantages over United's Boeing 247s were clearcut and the TWA-Douglas partnership ushered in a new era in air transport.

In June, 1937, TWA introduced the Douglas Sleeper Transport (DST), a variant of the DC-3, as shown on this July 1st, 1937, timetable. The new DC-3 was used also as a day plane, which TWA called the "Sky Club". It carried 21 passengers instead of the 14 of the DC-2, but with lower unit costs, a boon to profits.

**TWA baggage label**

**"The Lindbergh Line" was still used in advertising, to reflect Col. Lindbergh's services as Technical Adviser to TWA.**

**A revision of the baggage label was made later, to reflect the all-out campaign to publicize TWA as the fastest Coast-to-coast air line.**

The 4-engined Boeing 307, the Stratoliner, was introduced by TWA in July, 1940. This August 1st, 1940, timetable, now says "Largest ... fastest ... coast-to-coast" instead of the old slogan "Shortest ... fastest ...". Indeed it was the largest in U.S. domestic service, carrying 33 passengers in daytime service. The cabin was pressurized. Cruising altitude was 14,000 feet, an improvement over the DC-3's performance.

TWA used five of these Stratoliners in pre-WW II service, before they were transferred to government transoceanic service. Although the prototype had crashed, no problems had been encountered in all their service with TWA.

**TWA Stratoliner baggage label**

From the beginning of World War II until the present, TWA of course issued many brochures and timetables covering their DC-4s, Constellations, Stratocruisers, and several types of jet aircraft; there were just too many to fit into this book, which aims to cover only the pre-WW II era.

TWA issued many beautiful timetables and brochures over the years, but probably none more colorful than this one, January-February of 1939. The Douglas Skysleeper, Skyclub, and Skyliner were all advertised in this timetable.

Connections to Boston via American Airlines, to Washington and Pittsburgh by Pennsylvania Central Airlines (PCA), to Minneapolis by Northwest Airlines (NWA), and to Seattle by NWA and United Air Lines were given on the main trunk route schedule, also transatlantic and transpacific connections via Pan American Airways.

**DC-3 baggage label of TWA**

The wartime timetables of TWA, from mid-1942 thru 1944, pictured this DC-3 on their covers, since the Stratocruisers were on military service.

WEST COAST AIR TRANSPORT began service in 1928 between Seattle, Portland, San Francisco, and Los Angeles. This brochure emphasized the safety of tri-motored aircraft. It proclaimed that "flying is an absolutely safe method of transportation". It also noted that "nothing should be thrown out of the windows." The aircraft illustrated is the little-known Bach Air Yacht trimotor.
(National Air and Space Museum collection)

This brochure from collection of the National Air and Space Museum

WEST COAST AIR TRANSPORT had beautiful brochures and baggage labels. Their Bach Air Yachts of 1928 were featured on this label and on the brochure shown on the previous page, but their description as "tri-motored super air pullmans" streches the imagination a little.

**The baggage label above and the brochure at left show the Fokker F-10A airplanes operated by the air line in 1929. The brochure says "Fokker Tri-Motored Planes Used Exclusively". After becoming a division of Union Air Lines, the air line was purchased by Western Air Express late in 1929, but sold again in 1931 to Pacific Air Transport.**

STANDARD AIR LINES

The FAIR WEATHER ROUTE

LOS ANGELES - PHOENIX TUCSON - DOUGLAS AND EL PASO

**This is just one of the colorful undated timetables issued by Standard Air Lines, which was operated by the Aero Corporation of California.**

Tri-Motor Fokker F-10A aircraft operated on this route from Los Angeles across Arizona to Tucson via Phoenix. In 1929 the route was extended to El Paso, Texas, as shown on this schedule.

Western Air Express purchased Standard in 1930.

Another example of the colorful brochures put out by Standard Air Lines. One of their Fokker F-VII aircraft is shown. Schedules inside show its air plane leaving Los Angeles at 8.00 AM, arriving at El Paso, Texas via Tucson and Phoenix, at 5.30 PM, in time to connect with the Texas and Pacific Railway train to the north and east at 7.15 PM.

## San Francisco — Los Angeles

*365 Miles — Three Hours*

WESTERN AIR EXPRESS was selected from all Am
Fund for Promotion of Aeronautics as the agency
passenger airway. F-TEN, the super-trimotored Fokker
airplanes ever built—were picked from offerings by ever
aircraft because they represented an advance of at least tv
To facilitate operations along the San Francisco-Los
vith the Department of Commerce and the Weather Burea
ways weather service ever devised—a service made i
v.
May 26, 1928, the model passenger airway was o
planes, each powered with three 425-horsep
ve passengers, easily maintained an ave
hour schedule. On Septeml

This 1928 timetable states (above) that the "F-TEN, the super-trimotored Fokker monoplanes – finest and fastest commercial airplanes ever built – were picked from offerings by every American manufacturer of Multi-motored aircraft because they represented an advance of at least two years over any other design."

The timetable/brochure states that on June 15th the flying boat service (of Pacific Marine Airways) between Los Angeles and Catalina Island had been taken over by Western Air Express and that three bi-motored amphibian sesquiplanes (S-38s) were purchased for this service.

The brochure also states that twelve-hour daylight passenger service between Los Angeles and Missouri River Points would be inaugurated early in 1929 by Western Air Express.

The interior of this October, 1929, brochure is as attractive as its cover. The tri-motor Fokker F-10 is featured. The brochure has beautifully-illustrated double-page maps for the routes San Francisco-Los Angeles, Los Angeles-Kansas City, Los Angeles to Catalina, and Los Angeles-Salt Lake City. A similar brochure, dated May, 1929, showed only the Kansas City-Los Angeles map. The promotional material of this period vividly illustrates Western Air Express's initiatives in expanding air service to the east and to key transcontinental connecting points. The insertion of as yet unserved cities strongly implies further ambitions, frustrated by the Postmaster General's grand plan. (see TWA).

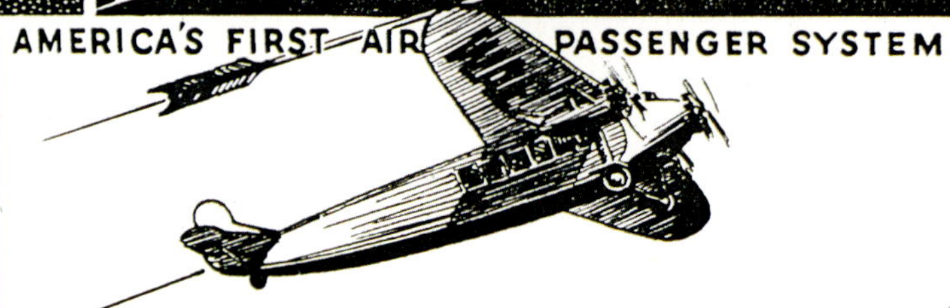


**CORRECTED TO JANUARY 1, 1932**

| | |
|---|---|
| Los Angeles | Denver |
| San Diego | Colorado Springs |
| Las Vegas | Pueblo |
| Chicago | Amarillo |
| Detroit | Cheyenne |
| Cleveland | Santa Fe |
| Omaha | Albuquerque |
| Pittsburgh | El Paso |
| New York | Washington |

Salt Lake City

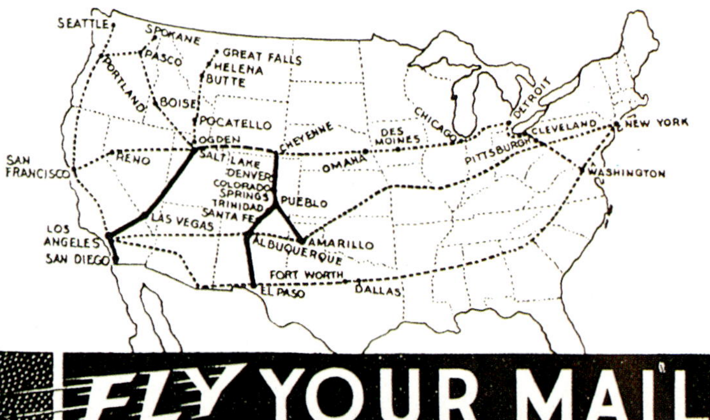


This January 1, 1932 timetable lists two divisions: San Diego-Los Angeles – Las Vegas-Salt Lake; and Cheyenne-Denver-Colorado Springs-Pueblo. Connections to other points in the U.S shown on the cover of this timetable were listed with other airlines: UAL, TWA, NPA, TAC and AA. Sadly, these two routes were the only remnants remaining of the once great Western Air Express, which could claim, early in 1930, to operate the biggest air line in the world.

WESTERN AIR EXPRESS first started service in 1926, and proudly claimed to be "America's oldest airline".

.It also claimed, in this timetable, to have established the first regularly scheduled passenger service in the United States in May, 1926, Los Angeles to Salt Lake City. That is obviously wrong, as the St. Petersburg-Tampa Airboat Line in 1914 and Aeromarine Airways in 1920-23 had regular scheduled daily passenger service, although in fairness, these were relatively short-lived enterprises.

The initial Douglas M-2 aircraft were soon replaced by Fokkers for passenger service, and in 1928 Fokker F-10 tri-motors were used on the Los Angeles to San Francisco route. Male stewards were used on the Fokkers. The airline claimed to be the first to use tri-motors (at least in the U.S.) and first to use flight attendants.

In 1929 West Coast Air Transport and Pacific Marine Airways were taken over, and in 1930 Standard Airlines was added to the system.

**Early WAE baggage label**
**The Fokker F-10**

NATIONAL PARKS AIRWAYS printed this undated timetable about 1928 when its air service started. Several undated timetables and brochures were issued before Jan. 1, 1932, the first one with an identifying date.

The Fokker Super-Universal is shown on the timetable. This six-seat air plane was used on the first routes from Great Falls to Helena, Butte, Pocatello, Ogden, and Salt Lake City.

By 1934 the Boeing 247 was being used, and ten passengers could be carried. Salt Lake City, Butte, and Helena were interchange points for connections with other carriers to all parts of the U.S.

In the summer of 1936 air tours of Yellowstone Park and Grand Teton were advertised at $7.50 for the one and a half hour scenic tour (a Boeing 80A trimotor was used). In the 1937 timetable the price had increased to $10.

**NPA baggage label.**
**In 1937 NPA was taken over by Western Air Express.**

WYOMING AIR SERVICE started flying in 1931. This undated timetable, probably from 1934 or 1935, shows schedules from Billings, Montana, south to Cheyenne, Wyoming, Denver, Colorado, and as far south as Pueblo.

From Pueblo connections were made with Varney Speed Lines to Las Vegas, Santa Fe, Albuquerque, and El Paso.

Connections at Cheyenne were made with United Air Lines to San Francisco and New York, and at Billings with Northwest Airlines to Seattle or Minneapolis.

Wyoming Air Service became Inland Air Lines in 1938.

**Gummed baggage label of Wyoming Air Service**

Here's another claimant to the title "World's Fastest Airline", also claimed by Bowen, Braniff Airways and Varney Speed Lines. All three airlines used the Lockheed Vega, which is shown on this 1929 timetable. One flight a day between Los Angeles and Reno was scheduled, Sundays excepted. The brochure said "Nevada Airlines Schedule for RENO-TONOPAH-LAS VEGAS line will be furnished upon request". The airline only lasted a year. The famous Col. Roscoe Turner was Chief Pilot and Manager of Operations.

First Edition, 1990
ISBN No. 0-961-8642-3-0
Library of Congress Catalogue Card No. 89-904-60
Manufactured in Singapore



Additional copies of this book or the three earlier volumes pictured below may be ordered for US$17.00 each, postpaid in the U.S. or Canada from:

DON THOMAS
1801 Oak Creek Drive
Dunedin, Fla., 34698, USA

Florida residents add $1.00 for state sales tax, please. Postpaid overseas by surface, $19.00 total; by air overseas $23.00 total per book.

---

**By the same author** — *NOSTALGIA PANAMERICANA* — Selling Romance in Color, a 64-page 9x12 book, every page in beautiful color, featuring the flying boats of Pan American Airways, its predecessors, associates, and contemporaries. The colorful art work of the early brochures and other advertising takes the reader back into the 1930s for a peek at the excitement created by early air travel, when flying was a thrill and an adventure for the passenger, and when the airlines were trying to convince the public of the safety and convenience of flight. The foreword is by R.E.G. Davies of the Smithsonian's National Air and Space Museum.

*LINDBERGH AND COMMERCIAL AVIATION.* This is a review of Col. Lindbergh's association as technical adviser with TAT, TAT-MADDUX, TWA and Pan American Airways in the 1930s. 40 colorful pages, 9x12 of Lindbergh memorabilia, including seldom-seen photographs of Charles and Anne Lindbergh, Igor Sikorsky, Basil Rowe, Juan Trippe, Amelia Earhart, and others. Also shown are many pioneer flight covers and other publicity which confirmed Lindbergh's invaluable contribution to these airlines.

*POSTER ART OF THE AIRLINES* — 64 pages of the most artistic airline posters of the 1920s to 1970s. The large 9x12 pages show off the beautiful colors of these rare posters to the best advantage, with accompanying text. PAN AMERICAN AIRWAYS is featured, along with its associates and contemporary competitors, U.S. and foreign. PANAGRA, CAT, PANAIR, CNAC, United, Braniff, ZEPPELIN, TWA, Imperial, KLM, and others are shown, with many vintage aircraft, Douglas twins, Constellations, Fokkers, and Fords. Foreword by R.E.G. Davies of the Smithsonian's NASM.